THE

ARTHURIAN

TRADITION

THE
ELEMENT
LIBRARY

THE
ARTHURIAN
TRADITION

JOHN MATTHEWS

ELEMENT
Shaftesbury, Dorset
Rockport, Massachusetts
Brisbane, Queensland

Published in Great Britain 1994 by
ELEMENT BOOKS LIMITED
SHAFTESBURY, DORSET

Published in the USA in 1994 by
Element Inc.
42 Broadway, Rockport, MA 01966

Published in Australia in 1994 by
Element Books Limited for
Jacaranda Wiley Limited
33 Park Road, Milton, Brisbane, 4046

ISBN 1-85230-567-3

Designed and created by
THE BRIDGEWATER BOOK COMPANY
Art Director *Annie Moss*
Designer *James Lawrence*
Managing Editor *Anna Clarkson*
Editors *Viv Croot, Carol McKendrick*
Picture Research *Vanessa Fletcher*

Printed and bound in Great Britain

British Library Cataloguing-in-Publication Data available

Library of Congress Cataloguing-in-Publication
Data available

CONTENTS

INTRODUCTION
What is the Arthurian Tradition? • *page 6*

1

THE HIGH KING
Arthur in History and Myth • *page 10*

2

MERLIN AND THE PROPHECIES OF THE LAND
Vision and Enchantment at Camelot • *page 22*

3

THE ROUND TABLE
Adventure in the Forest of the Mind • *page 32*

4

GODDESSES AND GUIDES
Morgan le Fay and the Otherworldly Women • *page 41*

5

LANCELOT AND TRISTAN
True Love and Perfect Chivalry • *page 50*

6

THE GRAIL QUEST
Spirituality and the Search for Absolutes • *page 62*

7

AVALON AND THE FAERY REALMS
Paths to the Land Beyond • *page 72*

8

THE UNENDING SONG
Arthur in the Modern World • *page 78*

GLOSSARY OF ARTHURIAN CHARACTERS • *page 86*
BIBLIOGRAPHY • *page 92*
ACKNOWLEDGEMENTS • *page 94*
INDEX • *page 95*

INTRODUCTION

What is the Arthurian Tradition?

The quintessence of chivalry, the Arthurian knights armed themselves to depart in search of heroic deeds and holy quests, undertaken for their own honour and to win the love of their ladies.

❖

Stories of adventure, of magic and romance are the stuff of the Arthurian tradition, which draws its energy from many sources. From the intricately woven fabric of Celtic myth and legend came the tales of Arthur and Avalon, of Merlin and the Grail, of the Otherworldly women who were its guardians. From the great chivalric epics of the Middle Ages came the stories of the Round Table knights: Lancelot and Galahad, Perceval and Gareth, Gawain and Lamorack, whose adventures filled literally thousands of manuscript pages relating their journeys through the dark, impenetrable forests of the Arthurian world. From the complex ethic of

Courtly Love, defined like a religious code, came a new attitude to women, who were no longer seen as chattels to be bought and sold in the matrimonial market-place of feudal Europe, but as potential goddesses all. This gave rise to such women as Guinevere, Isolde, Elaine of Astolat and Dindraine, and to the legion of ladies wooed and won, rescued and championed, by the knights who loved them.

Behind this, underpinning the whole mighty structure, lay a deeper dimension, drawn from a heritage of magical tradition, seeded by countless generations until it burst forth in the flowering of literature throughout the Middle Ages. Here, the themes which had dominated the inner lives of mankind from the Dreamtime before history, found a place. The eternal interaction of the Otherworld with our own dimension forms a constant backdrop to the tales of Arthur and his heroes, of their loves and their adventures. The secrets of immortality, of harmony with the earth, of true love and spiritual fulfilment, were only some of the rich gifts offered to these wandering men and women, who appear and disappear in an ever more bewildering fashion in the thronging scenes of countless texts.

Strange and terrible were the adventures they undertook; as strange and terrible as their adversaries: magicians and enchantresses, boiling waters and wild beasts with the intelligence of a man, serpents that turned into beautiful women if anyone dared to kiss them, invisible foes who struck from nowhere, demons, ghosts and knights whose armour changed colour in the blink of an eye. Even the landscape was unearthly, with underwater bridges able to change their form, fountains which ran with blood, trees one half in flame, the other in green leaf, wasted lands, which grew green again at a single word.

Magical rings, weapons, horses and bridles, swords pulled from stones that floated on water, ships that sailed by themselves and chess pieces moved by unseen hands – these are but a few of the elements which go to make up the world of the Arthurian tradition. Some we will meet in these pages, others we may seek out among the countless tales which make up the 'Matter of Britain'.

Above all, it should be recognised that these are not simply stories. Within them lies a depth and variety of human experience which derives from a timeless dimension. Taken as part of the continuing Western mystery tradition, they form a background to daily living in a unique and extraordinary way. Myths are timeless and cannot be defined or pigeon-holed to suit individual inclination.

ABOVE Arthur was linked to the magical and Otherworldly from his birth, when he was handed over to Merlin in secret at the gates of Tintagel castle.

❖

FAR LEFT Arthur's knights were often protected from evil by supernatural powers. Here, an angel guards Sir Guyon until he is rescued by his squire, who is also a monk.

❖

THE
ELEMENT
LIBRARY
THE
ARTHURIAN
TRADITION

Yet they are for all, as that wise mythologer Pamela Travers noted:

❧

The myths never have a single meaning, once and for all and finished. They have something greater; they have meaning itself. If you hang a crystal sphere in the window it will give off light from all parts of itself. That is how the myths are; they have a meaning for me, for you, and for everyone else.

❧

Meditating upon the images and events of the Arthurian legend can deepen an awareness of their inner transformative potential[34] 'The Arthurian Tarot[56] offers a unique approach to the inner quest through contemplation of the Arthurian archetypes and landscapes.

Finally, while I have ranged widely among the multitude of Arthurian texts, one in particular has been central to the creation of this book. This is Sir Thomas Malory's great work *Le Morte D'Arthur*,[47] which as a late work, written in 1485, not only sums up much of what had gone before, but also makes it accessible. Malory's uniqueness lies in his individuality and independence, which gave him the freedom to shape and adapt the

RIGHT *One of Arthur's many strange and terrible deeds was the slaying of the giant of Mont St Michel. As the King sailed across to Brittany, he dreamed of a boar vanquishing a dragon, which signified the coming conflict. One of Arthur's titles was 'The Boar of Cornwall.'*

❖

stories according to a personal vision of the 'high order of Chivalry'. He is also a great stylist, whose words are unforgettably poignant and charged.

Throughout this book therefore, I have taken Malory as a primary source and have not hesitated to paraphrase his words as though they were my own. I have endeavoured to make what flows more of a meditation on, rather than a history of, the subject. Those wishing to go more deeply into the question

ABOVE *Arthur was known all over Europe. This statue is from Innsbruck, Austria.*

❖

❖

LEFT *Arthur's Nemesis was Mordred, who was either his son or his nephew. Both combatants were mortally wounded in the fight.*

of the Arthurian tradition can do no better than read Malory, supplemented by the romances of Chrétien de Troyes,[8] *The Mabinogion*[46] and the English Gawain cycle.[23] Other, less familiar works, are referred to at appropriate points in the text, or in the bibliography at the end of the book. The emphasis throughout this book is on the imaginal dimension, since this is a vital part of what is, to this day, a *living* tradition.

RIGHT *Lancelot, the greatest of Arthur's knights, destined to become part of an eternal triangle with Arthur and Guinevere. Here he is seen with Elaine of Astolat, who died of unrequited love for him.*

❖

THE
HIGH KING

Arthur in History and Myth

*W*ither has not flying fame spread and familiarised the name of Arthur the Briton, even as
far as the empire of christendom extends? Who, I say, does not speak of Arthur the Briton,
since he is almost better known to the peoples of Asia than to the Britanni (Welsh and Cornish), as our
palmers returning from the East inform us? The Eastern peoples speak of him, as do the Western, though
separated by the width of the whole earth. . . Rome, queen of cities, sings his deeds, nor are Arthur's wars
unknown to her former rival Carthage, Antioch, Armenia, Palestine celebrate his acts.

Alanus de Insulis

THE CELTIC HERO

Arthur is a Celtic hero and it as a Celt and thus part of the Celtic world that he should be seen. No matter how far removed in time and culture the stories may take him, we should never allow ourselves to forget that they were a product of Celtic society, and that this point of origin continued to be felt long after Arthur had become recognised as a Christian king, with a band of heroes who met at a Round Table and spent their time in pursuit of adventure and love.

Arthur's historical origins are themselves shrouded in myth. The legends tell us that he was the son of King Uther Pendragon and the Lady Igraine of Cornwall, and that his birth was made possible through the magical arts of the magician Merlin, who later became his advisor in all things. History allows him no such 'romantic heritage' it grants him no

known parents, no wizard counsellor and no band of shining knights. What it does suggest is, in its own way, just as remarkable.

Arthur was born, so far as we can tell, sometime in the fifth or sixth century, either in Wales, the Midlands or Cornwall, and he became, not a great king, but an equally great war-leader, with the title *Dux Brittanorum*, Duke of Britain. As such, he commanded the armies of the various petty kings and chieftains, who had reasserted their claims to the land after the last vestiges of Roman rule came to an end in the previous century. Endlessly quarrelling, continuously raiding each other's lands for the sheer sport of it, they would have fallen easy victims to incoming invaders from Germany and Freisia, had it not been for Arthur, who persuaded the warring factions to fight against a common foe and to place him at the head of a united army.

How Arthur persuaded them is not recorded, as are few of his subsequent deeds. He seems to have led a band of mounted cavalry, perhaps the original 'Knights of the Round Table', whose mobility enabled them

THE
ELEMENT
LIBRARY
THE
ARTHURIAN
TRADITION

to strike deep into the territory overrun by
their enemies, withdraw as swiftly as they had
come and appear again many miles distant to
strike at another foe. Such tactics – learned,
perhaps, from Roman military methods –
must have given Arthur and his men almost
magical standing among both their own forces
and those of their enemy. It must have been
then that the first stirrings of the legendary
tales began.

Later writers recorded the still-potent
presence of Arthur, in the many places named
after him: Arthur's Seat, Arthur's Stone,
Arthur's Oven. A gravestone marked the
grave of his son, Anir; if it was moved during
one day, the next found it back in its original
place. A rocky outcrop bore the print of his
faithful hound, Cabal.

A series of great battles was recorded, their
sites now difficult, if not impossible, to
identify. We hear how Arthur, bearing a shield
with the image of the Virgin Mary painted

upon it, led his warriors against the Saxons to such good effect, that what began as an invasion ended as a more or less peaceful settlement. The invaders, were penned within certain areas of the country where they were able to farm the land and, in time, intermarry – thus founding the people known as the English, a mixture of Celt and Saxon which remained unchanged until the coming of the Normans in the eleventh century.

This was all to have a profound effect on the subsequent history of Arthur. The Britons, who fled the incoming Saxon invaders, found sanctuary across the sea in Brittany, opening up a channel which enabled the transmission of tales related orally – including, we must believe, tales about Arthur – which were the tales returned, in the form of stories and songs told by Anglo-Norman conteurs some 500 years later, became the foundation of the medieval romances of Arthur, on which most of the tradition is based.

OPPOSITE TOP *One of the many places associated with the King, Arthur's Stone, is at Cefn Bryn on the Gower Peninsula of West Glamorgan, Wales.*

❖

RIGHT *Another alleged physical reminder of Arthur's presence is King Arthur's footprint on Tintagel Island, Cornwall.*

❖

LEFT *The battle of Camlann, one of the few incidents of Arthur's life which appear in historical documents, took place around AD 540. Some authorities place site of the battle in Cornwall, and legend has it that Arthur rested and dined before the battle at Pendour Cove, shown here.*

❖

THE
ELEMENT
LIBRARY
THE
ARTHURIAN
TRADITION

THE ROMANTIC KING

The first writer consciously to draw on the still large oral sources pertaining to Arthur, was a twelfth-century 'historian' named Geoffrey of Monmouth. He it was who created a vehicle for the seemingly inexhaustible supply of stories concerning the exploits of Arthur and his heroes by writing a *History of the Kings of Britain*,[20] which though it also deals with such semi-historical figures as King Lear, Cassivellaunus and Constantine, allocates more than half the work to the lives of Arthur and Merlin.

Geoffrey's book became a best-seller of its time, with countless manuscript copies being made and distributed throughout England and the rest of Europe. Although his veracity as an historian was attacked, even by his near-contemporaries who referred to him as a 'fabulator' and 'writer of lies', there is more than a kernel of truth in what Geoffrey wrote. He claimed to have partially 'translated' an ancient book in the British tongue, although no trace of this has ever been discovered.

Whatever the truth Geoffrey pulled together strands of oral tradition, historical memory, and pure invention and dressed them in the fashions and settings of the time. In doing so, he created the first 'Arthurian' novel and set the seal upon the literary career of his hero for several ages to come. Here is part of his description of Arthur's court – which shows how far we have come from the setting of 'Dark Age' Britain:

ⴰⴰ

When the fest of Whitsuntide began to draw near, Arthur ... made up his mind to hold a plenary court at that season and place the crown of the kingdom on his head. He decided, too, to summon to this feast the leaders who owed him homage, so that he could celebrate Whitsun with greater reverence and renew the closest possible pacts of peace with his chieftains.

ⴰⴰ

LEFT *Arthur had strong connections with north-west France and fought a legendary battle with the giant of Mont St Michel, who had abducted Helena, the niece of King Hoel of Brittany.*

The feast is held at the City of Legions, Caerleon on Usk, and kings and chieftains come from all over Britain, from much of Europe, and from Scandinavia, which Arthur has recently conquered. All attend Mass in two great cathedral churches and afterwards there is a splendid feast, at which Kay the Seneschal, attended by a thousand noblemen dressed in ermine, bore in the food. Geoffrey goes on:

❧

If I were to describe everything, I should make this story far too long. Indeed, by this time, Britain had reached such a standard of sophistication that it excelled all other kingdoms in its general affluence, the richness of its decorations, and the courteous behaviour of its inhabitants. Every knight in the country who was in any way famed for his bravery wore livery and arms showing his own distinctive colour; and women of fashion often displayed the same colours. They scorned to give their love to any man who had not proved himself three times in battle. In this way the womenfolk became chaste and more virtuous and for their love the knights were ever more daring.

Already we have here a medieval, Christian court with its knights seeking to impress the ladies with their prowess in battle, the splendid banquets and great churches. This is no far cry from the romances which were to follow, and which established Arthur as the most important, most widely celebrated king in the Western world.

Geoffrey's work was taken up and translated from the original Latin into both Norman French and Anglo-Saxon. One of these translators, an Anglo-Norman named Wace, added the idea of the Round Table, at which all men sat in equality. A veritable avalanche of romances followed, the most famous of which were written, somewhere towards the end of the twelfth century, by a poet from Toyes in France named Chrétien. It is to him that we must look for the boldest conception of the stories which coloured most of the retellings that followed.

From his prolific pen flowed a series of five verse tales: *Erec and Enid, Cliges, Lancelot, Yvain* and *The Story of the Grail*.[8] Within these, much of what we now recognise as the essential core

ABOVE *Dagonet,
the jester of Camelot
whose wit and amiable
mockery earned him a
knighthood.*

❖

BELOW *South Cadbury
Castle, Somerset,
a possible site for the
legendary court
of Camelot.*

THE
ELEMENT
LIBRARY

THE
ARTHURIAN
TRADITION

of the Arthurian legends came into being. Chrétien gave us the stories of Arthur's greatest knights, the love affair of Lancelot and Arthur's queen and the quest for the Grail. Although these stories must have existed earlier in the form of oral tales, it is to Chrétien that we are indebted for the first versions recorded in writing.

His works are thronged with Otherworldy or primitive Celtic characters: Edern, son of Nut (Yder), Gilvaethwy, son of Don (Griflet), Gwalchmai (Gawain), who was the Knight of the Goddess, Maelwas (Maheolas) and Guigomar. In *Erec and Enid* it is notable that Arthur is seen as maintaining, or reviving, the ancient magical custom of the hunt for the White Stag. The hero who succeeded in killing this wondrous beast awarded its head to his lady and thus proclaimed her the fairest among all the women of the court. This theme, with its attendant episode of the kiss bestowed upon the winner, harks back to more primitive origins, where the hero married an ancient hag who afterwards transformed herself into a doe and the hero into a buck.

Even Chrétien's *Lancelot*, which on one level tells an elaborate and decorous tale of courtly love, in which the hero rescues his mistress

from the hands of a desperate man, is based on an earlier Celtic story contained in a sixth-century life of St. Gildas. Here the protagonist is a lord of the Otherworld who carries off Guinevere, not simply out of desire for her, but because she stands for the Sovereignty of the Land – an ancient idea which saw Arthur as inheriting his kingdom through marriage to an earthly representative of the Goddess.

Three of the stories retold by Chrétien appear in the *Mabinogion*, a collection of ancient Welsh tales collected and written down during the Middle Ages.[46] Debate has raged for a number of years as to which versions are the oldest. It now seems certain that Chrétien wrote his down first. Whoever the anonymous author of the three tales in the Welsh manuscripts may have been, he almost certainly drew on the same original source as the French Poet, although unlike Chrétien he retained many features of a more primitive nature. These versions of *Erec, Yvain* and *The Story of the Grail* therefore, actually represent earlier versions: Erec becomes Geraint, Yvain is called Owein and the spotless hero of the Grail story, Perceval, is replaced by Peredur, while all of the stories are cast in a more primitive mould.

Elsewhere in the same collection we find Arthur displaying further Celtic attributes. In the story of *Culhwch and Olwen*, we are given a glimpse of an Arthurian court probably not far removed from the sixth-century one – although Arthur has already become a 'king' and his warriors are more than slightly touched with the magical abilities of myth and legend. An astonishing list of heroes numbers over 250, many of whom possess attributes of a different kind to those one might expect to find among the putative 'Knights of the Round Table'.[62] There were, for example:

❖

BELOW *In Arthurian legend, a white doe or white stag often appeared to lead knights to adventures deep within the forest.*

Gila Stag Shank, who could leap three hundred acres in a single bound . . . Gweveyl son of Gwastad (when he was sad he would let one lid droop to his navel and raise the other until it was a hood over his head), . . . Gwrhr Interpreter of Tongues, who knew all tongues. . . Cust son of Clustveinydd (were he buried seven fathoms in the earth he would hear an ant stirring from its bed fifty miles away).[46]

❖❖❖

Thus the magnetic figure of Arthur drew to him a vast panoply of Celtic heroes, for who it was an honour to serve at his court. Of many, we now know nothing more than their names; yet some are familiar. Kai (the later Sir Kay), Bedwyr (better known as Sir Bedivere), and Owein (the Sir Ywain of French and English romances) have their place among the fantastic cavalcade of Otherworldly characters, while Arthur himself remains the outstanding figure, cloaked in the majesty and mystery of the Celtic world.

In *Culhwch and Olwen* Arthur must also give gifts when asked for in a certain way – though he may occasionally make exceptions:

You shall have the request that head and tongue name . . . excepting only my ship, my mantle, my sword Caledvwich, my spear Rhongomynyad, my shield Wynebgwrthucher, my knife Carnwennan and my wife Gwenhwyvar.[46]

This list of Otherworld weaponry shows that Arthur himself had by this stage acquired Otherworldly origins, or that he had 'stolen' them. Evidence of this is to be found in an early Welsh poem called *Preiddeu Annwn,*[45] *Spoils of the Underworld.* In this Arthur leads a band of warriors on a raid into the realm of the dead to steal the Cauldron of Arawn, which could restore to life any dead warrior placed within it.

More than just another adventure lies behind this. It is evident that Arthur, by acquiring this trophy, also acquired for himself something of the power of the Lord of the Otherworld. Thus we are not surprised to find him, in another story, ordering the exhumation of the head of Bran, the great guardian spirit of Britain, on the grounds that he alone, Arthur Pendragon, should defend the island.

The great Celticist Jean Markale sees in these episodes indication of a conflict between Arthur and the Lords of the Otherworld; hence the number of magicians and enchantresses to be found visiting the Otherworld with the object of testing both Arthur himself and all his knights. Perhaps

also we may see evidence of another inheritance, both racial and religious, in the number of queens and Otherworldly women who represent, in some sort, the presence of goddesses once worshipped in these islands.

The literary career of Arthur continued unabated for another 300 years, with countless new stories and retellings appearing throughout Britain and Europe. New characters appeared, or became attracted into the Arthurian ambience. Celtic warriors, such as Gwalchmai and Lleminawg, traded their old names and customs for new, and as 'Gawain' and 'Lancelot' became the most widely known and written about characters in the whole of Western courtly literature.

The portraits of Arthur were not always flattering. In several early chronicles he is given the epithet *Horribilus* and described as a

ABOVE *Memories of earlier Celtic heroes helped shape the character and deeds of Arthur. One such was Cuchulainn, the champion of Ulster.*
BELOW *Tom Thumb, said to be Arthur's favourite dwarf, was often at the Round Table. His birth – and size – had been predicted by Merlin.*

H C

THE
ELEMENT
LIBRARY
THE
ARTHURIAN
TRADITION

ABOVE *Oberon, the King of the Faeries, was reputed by some sources to be the child of Morgan le Fay and Julius Caesar.*

❖

slothful state from which more than one effort has to be made to rouse him.

Yet despite these (comparatively minor) shortcomings, Arthur remains the shining example of all that a Christian king should be. When William Caxton published his edition of Thomas Malory's *Le Morte d'Arthur* in 1485, he described in his preface how numerous people had reproached him with failing to print a history of 'the most renowned Christian King . . . Arthur, which ought to be remembered among us English men to fore of all other Christian kings'.

Malory's book retold the story of Arthur from birth to death, in prose which has seldom been equalled. It was a threnody for the dying age of chivalry, which Arthur and his knights above all represented. It has ensured that the stories of the noble Fellowship of the Round Table have not been forgotten, and that the tradition they embody has remained evergreen.

tyrant. In later romances he falls for a Saxon enchantress, lives for two and a half years with a twin half-sister of Guinevere who has been substituted for the real queen (this is made the excuse for Lancelot and the real Guinevere to become lovers), and generally falls into a

THE MYTHIC HERO

Far more than the memory of a great and heroic leader was being recorded. More ancient memories were stirred to life by the deeds of the historical Arthur than were recorded in the romances or the pseudo-histories. Beneath these, as beneath the level of the Celtic stories, existed a further dimension – an older, deeper set of mythically conceived archetypes, which become forged by time and circumstance into a cycle which has stood the test of the ages and continues to affect anyone who encounters it.

From time to time we catch a glimpse of these mighty figures behind the patina of Celtic or medieval legends, as in the story of *The Dream of Rhonabwy*, from the *Mabinogion*. Here, Rhonabwy, who may well have lived in thirteenth-century Wales, falls asleep on a magical ox's hide which induces in him a dream of the mythical past. He sees himself and his companions riding across a plain, where they encounter Iddawg, son of Mynyo, who is described as follows:

❧✣

He saw a young man with curly hair and a newly trimmed beard riding a yellow horse. This man was green from the tops of his legs and his kneecaps down, and wore a tunic of yellow brocade sewn with green thread; on his thigh was a gold-hilted sword, with a scabbard of new cordovan and a gold buckle. Over the tunic he wore a mantle of yellow brocade sewn with green silk, and the green of the rider's outfit and his horse's was the colour of fir needles, while the yellow was the colour of broom. His bearing was so awesome that they became frightened and fled, but he gave chase; when his horse breathed out they drew ahead, but when it breathed in they were as near as its chest.[46]

❧✣

If we were in any doubt that this represents the first stage of a fully fledged mythic scenario, this is confirmed by the remainder of the story, as Rhonabwy and his companions meet successive members of Arthur's war-band and finally the king himself. When Iddawg presents Rhonabwy, Arthur's reaction is first to ask where he found these 'little men', and then to bemoan the fate of the land for 'being in the care of such puny men . . . after that sort that held it before'.

All great heroes may seem like giants to the mortal who enters the otherworld, but this is because they are mythic archetypes, drawn from the deepest levels of the human imagination.

We find further indication of this a little later in the same text, where Arthur and his nephew Owein play a game of *gwyddbwyll*, which is akin to chess and possesses profound symbolic qualities. While they are playing, a battle begins between Owein's 'ravens' and Arthur's men and a succession of messengers appears to report increasing degrees of carnage on both sides. With either Arthur or Owein requesting the withdrawal of forces, and each time the response is the ritualised formula 'Play on', until at last Arthur's anger is such that he crushes the game pieces to golden dust, whereat the combat ceases as abruptly as it had begun.

ABOVE *Lugh the Sun God, father of Cuchulainn, plays a symbolic game of chess, just as Arthur played with Owein.*

❖

This strange contest has many levels of meaning. Owein's ravens are really Otherworldly women who possess the ability to transform their shape; they are the sisters of Owein's mother or aunt, the goddess Modron, who conforms both to the archetype of the Great Mother and to that of Sovereignty, the tutelary goddess of the land. So at another level, the battle between Arthur and his nephew may be interpreted as a struggle for the rulership, the sovereignty of the inner land of Britain. It is, perhaps, an annual event, which continues to take place in the Otherworld even though Arthur has himself long been withdrawn from the world of men.

For the king, like all great mythic heroes, is deathless. At the end of his earthly career, after the great battle of Camlan (site unknown) in which he fights against his own son, Mordred, Arthur receives a wound beyond the skills of mortal healing. But there comes the enchantress Morgan le Fay, Arthur's half-sister, who until that moment had been his implacable enemy. After searching the wound

LEFT *Mortally wounded after his battle with Mordred, Arthur is borne away by Morgan le Fay, his enemy in life and his protector in the afterlife.*

❖

THE
ELEMENT
LIBRARY
THE
ARTHURIAN
TRADITION

ABOVE *Stories from Arthurian legend were current in Geoffrey Chaucer's time (c 1345-1400). Gawain and Lancelot are given as examples of the 'very parfit gentle knight' and the Wife of Bath tells the tale of the Loathly Lady, identified with Ragnall the wife of Gawain.*

❖

OPPOSITE *Jousting at Camelot, Arthur's court of heroes, at once real and archetypal.*

she takes him away in her magical boat to Avalon, the island paradise of the Celts, to be healed and to await a future call to his country's need.

Thus Arthur conforms in every detail to the mythic archetype. Strangely born, his end is mysterious. His relationship with the Goddess of the land and her avatars is established early. He summons a great fellowship of heroes to sit at his circular table which echoes, as Merlin says, 'the roundness of the world', and also the circle of the heavens. He is placed in polarised balance by the presence of Morgan, who acts always against him until the end, then appears as his guardian and protectress. He possesses magical weapons – in particular, of course, the sword Excalibur, which must be returned to the lake when he no longer

requires it. With his going, the world is a
lesser place; though his dream of a unified,
perfected earthly kingdom, remains, to be
taken up and renewed throughout time to our
own days, and doubtless beyond.

In the great romances, which added
successive dimensions to Arthur's career,
drawing in the great cycle of the Grail, and
annexing the adventures of many individual
heroes until these formed a constellation
around the central star that was Arthur, we
may see a dream being worked out. It is not
simply Merlin's dream of a unified, earthly
kingdom expressing the highest values known
to man; it is the encapsulated desire of an age
that, even in its most violent moments,
consistently sought to reach upward to heaven
and touch the hand of God.

The Arthurian Dream is, in the end, an
expression of all that is best in what Sir
Galahad, in Thomas Malory's great book,
called 'this unstable world'. That the
Arthurian tradition continues to stand for
these things is all the indication we should
need as to its enduring validity and
extraordinary power.

ABOVE *Arthur's first
sight of the lake-borne
Excalibur, his magical
weapon. At the end of
his life, it was returned
to the water.*

❖

2

MERLIN
AND THE PROPHECIES
OF THE LAND

Vision and Enchantment at Camelot

*Merlin with the kings
Ban, Bors and Arthur.
He was sage and advisor
to all three.*

❖

*A*nd those who knew Merlin well and who had served Uther Pendragon came to the king and said
to him; 'Sire, honour Merlin greatly for he was a good prophet for your father and has always
loved your family much. And he foretold to Vertiger his death and it was he who had the
Round Table made. Now see to it that he is well honoured, for you will never ask him about
anything that he will not tell you.' And Arthur responded that thus he would do.

Didor Perceval

The Vortigern Prophecy

~

Vortigern, a minor king, makes a bid for power by bringing in Saxon mercenaries to fight the Picts in the north and his own enemies elsewhere. He is briefly popular, but his star soon wanes as more and more Saxons arrive and begin acquiring larger and larger areas of land. Finally, the exiled sons of the former High King of Britain return at the head of an army and Vortigern flees to Wales, where he intends to build a stronghold. Having chosen a site, he sets his builders to work; but every night the progress they have made is undone by a mysterious agency. Vortigern consults his druids and learns that only the blood of a fatherless child, spilled on the stones, will ensure the completion of the fortress. Sent out to search for such a child, Vortigern's soldiers discover Merlin at Carmarthen (said by Geoffrey to derive from *Caer Myrddin*, Merlin's Town). He is the son of a Welsh princess but no one knows his father. The woman and her son are brought before Vortigern, and Merlin's mother explains that she has led a devout and pure life, but that she was visited in her chamber by a golden being who fathered the child upon her. Vortigern is tempted to disbelieve this account but Merlin himself speaks out in defence of his mother, and challenges Vortigern and his druids to explain the real reason why the tower will not stand. Merlin tells them that there is a pool beneath the hilltop and that within it is a stone coffer containing two dragons, one red and the other white, who battle mightily every night, thus causing the ground to shake and the work of the king's masons to fall. Vortigern orders his men to dig and finds that all is as Merlin had foretold. The wise child then explains that the red dragon symbolises Britain and the white dragon the Saxons, and prophesies that after a time the white will overcome the red. He then goes into a trance and for the next twelve to fourteen pages in Geoffrey's book, proceeds to expound the future of the race unto the very end of time. In the process he prophesies the coming of Arthur, 'the Boar of Cornwall', which will 'bring relief from these invaders, for it will trample their necks beneath its feet', and warns Vortigern of his own forthcoming death. The end of this extraordinary outburst is apocalyptic, with references to riot among the planetary houses and the fall of deadly rain. Finally, in the twinkling of an eye the seas shall rise up and the arena of the Winds shall be opened once again. The Winds shall do battle together with a blast of ill-omen, making their din reverberate from one constellation to another.[20]

In Merlin's prophecy, the red and white dragons locked in mortal combat symbolised the grim power struggle between the Britons and the invading Saxons.

❖

THE
ELEMENT
LIBRARY
THE
ARTHURIAN
TRADITION

GOD OR DRUID?

Merlin first appears in recognisable form in the writings of the twelfth-century pseudo-historian Geoffrey of Monmouth, who may have heard stories of Merlin either during his childhood in Monmouth, or in his later days as Bishop of St Asaph in North Wales. Either way, Merlin plays a considerable role in his *History of the Kings of Britain*, and he also wrote (or compiled) a volume of Merlin's prophecies, which he incorporated into his larger work of the history of early Britain.

The veracity of Geoffrey's book has been the cause of scholarly debate for generations. While many earlier critics dismissed him as a flagrant forger, a more recent attitude tends to emphasise his value as a recorder of traditional tales and native folklore. R. J. Stewart, in his study of the Prophecies, has established that Geoffrey must have had access to a large collection of material which recorded Merlin's inspired utterances – although whether these were entirely genuine, or represented a Merlin tradition, has yet to be completely established.

Nowhere is the inner nature of the Arthurian Tradition more clearly focused than in the figure of Merlin. Advisor to three kings, prophet, magician, and wise man, his shadowy presence seldom takes any single form for long enough to observe his real nature. His genesis, within the 'Matter of Britain', is almost as complex.

One commentator has called him a god of the ancient native people of Britain; his home, at Maridunum, was also the site of his cult.[2] Others have seen in him a shaman or a wild man,[83] an inner guardian of the land[32] or a seer whose prophecies have a very real validity for our own time.[78] But he eludes any fixed definitions; his origins and his ultimate fate remains as mysterious as at the time of his first appearance. Even his own words do not enlighten but render him more opaque: 'Because I am dark, and always shall be, let my book be dark and mysterious in those places where I will not show myself'.[70]

The whole structure and content of Merlin's prophecies shows a remarkable grasp of the inner tides which control the fate of the world, and Merlin's vision of the future is as terrifying as anything foretold by the French seer Nostradamus or his ilk. Wherever Geoffrey found the material for this part of his book, it was clearly not from his own mind, indicating, as already stated, that he was in some way the recipient of a body of traditional lore associated with Merlin.[77]

Geoffrey himself, as we have seen, claimed that he was merely translating 'a certain very ancient book written in the British language', lent to him by Archdeacon Walter of Oxford, and that this was the source of all that he wrote. No trace of this book has ever come to light, and it has generally been considered to be an invention by Geoffrey to add veracity to his fanciful history. However, while there seems no reason why there should not have been such a book, it is evident that Geoffrey embellished his sources considerably. It is known that the source of the story of Merlin's prophecies are the writings of the eighth-century monk, Nennius, and his writings are possibly one of the few authentic records of

the Arthurian era. His youthful prophet was named Ambrosius, and it seems that in order not to confuse him with Ambrosius the son of Constantine, who overthrows Vortigern, Geoffrey borrowed the name of Merlin from an earlier native figure, Merddyn Wyllt 'the Wild', who may actually have lived either in Scotland or in Wales during the sixth or seventh century.[83]

This makes the prophet roughly contemporary with Arthur, and it is possible that we have here a genuine tradition of the great war-leader and his inspired advisor which has been carried through to reappear in Geoffrey's text in a mangled form.

Whatever the truth of the matter, it was to have a profound effect on the history of Merlin. Geoffrey's book, as we have seen, became a best-seller throughout the Middle Ages, and may well have given the initial impetus to the entire phenomenon of Arthurian literature. After the episode of Vortigern's tower and his first great prophetic outpouring, Merlin went on to perform several prodigious feats – including the moving of a ring of magical stones called 'The Giant's Dance' all the way from Ireland to Salisbury Plain in Wiltshire, where they became a vast mausoleum for the Kings of Britain, better known as Stonehenge.

ABOVE *Vortigern (ruled c 450), here seen dispatching some murderers to their death, was an historical figure whose existence is attested by the Welsh writer Nennius (fl796) and the Northumbrian monk Bede (c 673-735).*

THE
ELEMENT
LIBRARY
THE
ARTHURIAN
TRADITION

While Merlin was clearly not responsible for the building of the great megalithic monument, it is possible that even here Geoffrey was recording an ancient tradition which related to the original builders of the great stone circle. Merlin went on to serve both the sons of King Constantine, Ambrosius Aurelianus and Uther Pendragon who became the father of Arthur. It is to Geoffrey again that we owe the famous story of the hero's conception. Merlin magically disguises Uther to look like the husband of the Duchess of Cornwall, so that he can lie with her and beget the future king.

Subsequently, Merlin became advisor to Arthur, in which guise he is still best remembered, and which is how he appears in all the major versions of the story which follow Geoffrey's account. Merlin thus serves three kings and for each he performs remarkable feats, while serving as prophet and advisor. He is never pictured as a mere court magician however; there is always something restless and untamable about him, vestiges of a wild and Otherworldly dimension continue to cling to him, and for this also we owe something to Geoffrey of Monmouth.

ABOVE *This fantastic picture by John Martin, shows Merlin appearing on the cliffs above Conway castle in Wales.*

❖

LEFT *Stonehenge, the ancient site in Wiltshire associated with Druidic tradition. According to legend, the stones to build it were magically transported by Merlin, in his avatar as a Druid, either from Presilis in Wales, or from Ireland.*

THE LIFE OF MERLIN

Geoffrey was not finished with the character of Merlin. He wrote another book, in Latin verse, called the *Vita Merlini, The Life of Merlin* in which he extended his account of the famous prophet to an even greater degree. Here, he paints a very different picture from that of his earlier works. Merlin is a prince in his own right who, driven mad by the scenes of carnage at the battle of Arderydd, ran away and lived like a wild beast in the wilderness for many years before returning at last to sanity and becoming recognised as a great prophet and wise man.

Geoffrey was drawing again on the traditions surrounding the mysterious figure of Myrddin Wyllt, who seems to have lived in post-Arthurian Britain and to have absorbed something of an even earlier, possibly deified being, of great antiquity. Some of the writings of this historical Myrddin have actually survived and show him to have been no mean poet.

Myrddin's poem 'Apple Trees', is full of curious lore and the remains of the tradition which depicts Myrddin living wild among the woods with only a pig for company (the pig was regarded as a sacred beast among the Celts). It shows that, whatever else he may have been, Merlin (or Myrddin) was very much a part of the ancient bardic tradition of Wales. Together with those of Taliesin, Aneurin, and Llwyarch Hen, his writings form part of a significant body of literature which has survived (not without a good deal of reworking) to the present day. I have elsewhere undertaken a study of this tradition,[59] which proves to contain the last vestiges of native British shamanism. Although it is of a different tone to the accounts of Merlin's later career, many of his magical acts are duplicated in this more primitive strain of material.

By drawing together these elusive threads of tradition, Geoffrey provided a foundation on which many generations of writers could build. The wonder-working prophet of the *Historia* and the *Vita* proved immensely popular with the medieval audiences – as, indeed, he has continued to be. Numerous texts followed, which extended Merlin's role even further, until he became a central figure within Arthurian tradition.

Apples and apple trees were very significant in Celtic mythology.

Apple trees
~

SWEET APPLETREE THAT LUXURIANTLY GROWS!
FOOD I USED TO TAKE AT IS BASE TO PLEASE A FAIR MAID,
WHEN, WITH MY SHIELD ON MY SHOULDER, AND MY SWORD ON MY THIGH,
I SLEPT ALL ALONE IN THE WOODS OF CELYDDON.

HEAR, O LITTLE PIG! NOW APPLY THYSELF TO REASON,
AND LISTEN TO BIRDS WHOSE NOTES ARE PLEASANT,
SOVEREIGNS ACROSS THE SEA WILL COME ON MONDAY;
BLESSED WILL THE CYMRY [WELSH] BE FROM THAT DESIGN.
SWEET APPLETREE, WHICH GROWS BY THE RIVERSIDE!
WITH RESPECT TO IT, THE KEEPER WILL NOT THRIVE ON ITS SPLENDID FRUIT,
WHILE MY REASON WAS NOT ABERRANT, I USED TO BE AROUND ITS STEM.
WITH A FAIR SPORTIVE MAID, A PARAGON OF SPLENDID FORM.
TEN YEARS AND FORTY, AS THE TOY OF LAWLESS ONES,
HAVE I BEEN WANDERING IN GLOOM AND AMONG SPRITES...

SWEET APPLETREE, AND A TREE OF CRIMSON HUE,
WHICH GREW IN CONCEALMENT IN THE WOOD OF CELYDDON;
THEY SOUGHT FOR THEIR FRUIT, IT WILL BE IN VAIN,
UNTIL CADWALDYR COMES FROM THE CONFERENCE OF RHYD RHEON,
AND CYNON TO MEET HIM ADVANCES UPON THE SAXONS;
THE CYMRY WILL BE VICTORIOUS, GLORIOUS WILL BE THEIR LEADER.
ALL SHALL HAVE THEIR RIGHTS, AND THE BRYTHON WILL REJOICE,
SOUNDING THE HORNS OF GLADNESS, AND CHANTING THE SONG OF PEACE AND HAPPINESS!

Translated by W.F. Skene, *Four Ancient Books of Wales*

THE
ELEMENT
LIBRARY
THE
ARTHURIAN
TRADITION

THE DEVIL'S SON

Inevitably perhaps, with his being so talented in the reading of the stars and the future, Merlin became associated in the medieval consciousness with the idea of necromancy, and thus with the devil. When the twelfth-century Burgundian writer Robert de Borron, as he had previously done with the Grail legends (see Chapter 6), set about filling in some of the details of Merlin's history missing from the earlier records, he gave a very different account.

He described the demons of Hell plotting the birth of an Anti-christ – Merlin. They sent forth a minor demon of the kind known as a *succubus*, who was to overshadow an innocent Princess of Dyfed and father upon her a child of evil. Their plans are frustrated by the innate goodness of the child's mother, who finds a

ABOVE *Merlin appears as a stag: one of his many magical skills was his ability to change shape.*

❖

priest to baptise the infant before evil can take hold of him. He is born with a hairy pelt and the ability to speak and reason almost from birth. The hair falls from him when he is baptised, but he retains both the power of speech and an Otherworldly clairvoyance.

Thus Merlin's abilities are accounted for in terms acceptable to a Christian readership; the 'golden stranger' of the earlier tales becomes a demon, the 'god' a 'devil', and powers which would have been wholly appropriate to a Celtic god become magical and wondrous – the product of necromancy. Their effects remain the same, Merlin as magician reigns supreme.

Interestingly, Merlin's mother is described as a Princess of Dyfed, and in Geoffrey's *Vita Merlini*, we may remember, Merlin is also described as a prince in his own right. This seems to add yet one more strand to the complex web of associations. No record of a sixth-century noble named Merlin or Myrddin has come to light, but this does not mean that no such person existed. The overlay of mythical and historical figures is anyway so complete that it is no longer possible to differentiate one from the other.

In the same way, Merlin the prophet seems to have assumed some of the attributes and abilities of an inspired semi-mythical madman named Lailoken, who hailed from the Lowlands of Scotland at roughly the same period as Merlin may have flourished. Through this character Merlin derives certain aspects of the Scottish St Kentigern, whose history reflects that of the mage at several points, and who was instrumental in restoring Lailoken to sanity.

A story common to both Merlin and Lailoken concerns their laughter: in each instance they laugh three times at unlikely events, betraying their uncanny knowledge by so doing. Merlin laughs at the wife of his friend King Rhydderch when he sees a leaf caught in her hair – the heritage of an adulterous tryst; again at a beggar whom he knows to be sitting over a pot of gold; and a third time at a youth buying a new pair of shoes when in fact he is destined to die within the course of that very day.

The theme is an old one and derives ultimately from Oriental sources – as indeed do several other aspects of Merlin's career, prompting one commentator to suggest that his origins may have been further east than we have come to suspect. However, this only serves to show how closely Merlin came to conform to the image of the magician. In common with two other poets, the Celtic Taliesin and the Roman Virgil, his demonstrable knowledge of other levels of meaning and understanding earned him the title of magician. The prophetic element derived from Lailoken, or from more ancient records, and the final image of the many-faceted Merlin coalesced to become that of the wise and mystical magician and sagacious counsellor of Arthur's court.

Additional to this, is the idea of Merlin's shamanic background. Several traces of this remain, his ability to change shape at will (particularly into the form of a stag, a typical shamanic totem beast), his prophetic and inspired utterances, and the motif of the threefold death, identified by R. J. Stewart in his two books about Merlin.[77, 78]

Here, Merlin's sister Ganeida, to test his newly restored sanity, presents him with the same youth in three different guises. In each case Merlin predicts a different end for the youth, who will hang, drown and fall to his death. This prediction is fulfilled when the youth falls over a cliff, and is suspended by an ankle caught in a tree root with his head beneath the waters of a river.

In the story of mad Lailoken the prophet predicts the threefold death for himself, from which we may justly believe that the same thing once held good for Merlin also. The motif is an extremely ancient one, deriving ultimately from the self-initiation, or false-death, of the shaman. It reappears in esoteric symbolism in the tarot card of 'The Hanged Man', and signifies the relationship of the magician/shaman to the elements.

Although we are able to delineate these aspects of Merlin separately, the overall portrait remains consistent, suggesting a single figure. Even the manner of his departure from the world bears an overall similarity, despite surface differences.

Merlin was a many-sided figure – Druid, shaman, Christian monk, necromancer, magician, astronomer, youth and old sage. He was also a seer and a prophet, and his predictions always came true.

THE
ELEMENT
LIBRARY
THE
ARTHURIAN
TRADITION

MERLIN AND NIMUE

The reference to 'a fair sportive maid' in Myrddin's Apple Trees indicate the antiquity of a final theme. This is Merlin's fatal love for the fairy Nimue, sometimes called Niniane or Vivienne, who is portrayed as having stolen his power and then using it to bind him.

We first hear of Nimue in the Merlin section of the vast Arthurian compilation known as *The Vulgate Cycle*.[71] This massive compilation of story and polemic was written down during the first half of the thirteenth century by clerks belonging to the order of Cistercian monks, the order founded by the great medieval theologian Bernard of Clairvaux. While specifically Christianising the material, it also drew upon a vast range of earlier works, including one which gave a more complex rendition of Robert de Borron's *Merlin*.

In this quotation from *The Vulgate Cycle* we read of the forester Dionas, so named because of his devotion to the goddess Diana, who had a daughter named Niniane, of whom the goddess spoke the following prophecy:

I grant thee, and so doth the god of the sea and the stars . . . that the first female child that thou shalt have shall be much coveted by the wisest man that ever was on earth . . . and he shall teach her the most part of his wit and cunning by way of necromancy, in such manner that he shall be so desirous after he hath seen her, that he shall be powerless against her wish, and all things that she enquireth he shall teach.[71]

Niniane is thus in some sense regarded as under the aegis of the goddess, just as her father is described as her 'god-son', a euphemistic way of saying that he was a worshipper of Diana. As to the prophecy, it is proved to be accurate in the story, cited on the right, given here in the version by Malory.

This somewhat unflattering portrayal of the aged Merlin, besotted with the beautiful fairy damsel (one of the Ladies of the Lake no less!) who cozens his secrets out of him and then uses them to imprison him, seems to be part

Merlin fell in a dotage on one of the damosels of the lake, that hight Nimue. But Merlin would let her have no rest, but always he would be with her. And ever she made Merlin good cheer till she had learned of him all manner of thing that she desired; and he was assotted upon her ... and always ... lay about the lady to have her maidenhood, and she was ever passing weary of him, and fain would have been delivered of him because he was a devil's son ... And so on a time it happened that Merlin showed her a rock whereat was a great wonder ... So by her subtle working she made Merlin to go under that stone ... but she wrought ... for him that he came never out for all the craft that he could do. And so she departed and left Merlin.

(*Le Morte D'Arthur Bk IV, Ch. 1.*)

of the general tendency of certain medieval writers to seek a Christian interpretation of often quite primitive, pagan material. Thus Merlin himself becomes the son of a devil, rather than an Otherworldly being, and Nimue, whose father served the goddess Diana, is portrayed as a temptress whose power derives solely from that of Merlin.

The *Vita Merlini* portrays Merlin as having a sister, Ganeida, whose own wisdom is no less than his. When the moment comes for him to retire from the world, as it does to all high initiates, Merlin withdraws with Ganeida to a wonderful observatory with seventy-two windows, from which they observe the stars and hold lengthy philosophical discussions upon the meaning of creation. Perhaps we may look to this story for the origin of Nimue, transformed from sister to temptress, who thus has to extract the wisdom of Merlin by the use of her wiles. Even the portrayal of Merlin as a man stems from a misconception – nowhere is his age specifically stated, and he does, in fact, take the forms both of an old man and of a youth on more than one occasion.

Neither is it without significance that the last person to hear the voice of Merlin is another character who underwent similar downgrading with the works of predominantly Christian interpreters. This was Gawain who began life as the Champion of the Goddess and ended it as a murderer and a libertine.[59] Thus it seems wholly appropriate that, happening to pass by the great stone under which the image is imprisoned, Gawain hears 'the cry of Merlin'.

Afterwards, Merlin's tomb becomes known as the *Perron de Merlin* or Stone of Merlin and there the Knights of the Round Table meet to begin their adventures. Thus, even in his withdrawn state, Merlin may be said to influence the doings of the Arthurian world, and indeed the seeds he had planted in the early days of Arthur's reign are meant to prepare the way for the great Quest for the Holy Grail – though this was not to begin for many years after his departure.

Significantly, in another version of this story (from *The Romance of Perceval in Prose*), Merlin remarks that he must withdraw because: 'Those who are gathered together here must believe what they see happen and I would not that they should think that I had brought it about'.[70] Then, as now, the words of the *withdrawn* prophet meant more than those of the teacher in the flesh.

The most mysterious version of Merlin's departure is that which describes him as retreating into an *esplumoir*, a word which has no precise meaning but which is sometimes interpreted as referring to a 'moulting cage', a cage in which the hawks used in falconry are placed to shed their feathers. Symbolically, this seems clear enough: Merlin withdraws to shed the form of his current life and to adopt a new spiritual garment. From within his moulting cage, he is enabled to see far more than ever before, and his influence extends further, beyond the confines of the Arthurian Kingdom into the world at large. He remains, as the psychologist Carl Jung called him, 'the age-old son of the mother',[86] able to perceive the greatest depths and to work within the inner realms towards the integration of mankind with deity – the final aim of all such co-workers with God.

Merlin conforms at every level, then, to the powerful image of the inner master, the great soul who is able to participate at will in the outer history of creation. It is the presence of Merlin alone that lifts the Arthurian tradition far above the largely narrative levels of many similar sagas and legend cycles. In the next chapters, we shall examine further how this inner dimension impinges continually on the outer working of the stories.

OPPOSITE LEFT
Merlin and Nimue, or Vivienne, the wood goddess with whom he became besotted and who stole all his secrets from him.

❖

❖

BELOW *Sir Gawain confronts the mysterious Green Knight whose head he cut off at Arthur's court and who now demands Gawain's head in return. In the story of Gawain and the Green Knight the contest became a test of Gawain's purity and honour as well as a reflection of the Christian concept of redemption and renewal.*

3

THE
ROUND TABLE

Adventure in the Forest of the Mind

Arthur's marriage to Guinevere established his court. As her dowry, Guinevere brought the legendary Round Table and the royal couple became the centre of the glittering circle of chivalric knights.

❖

A rthur never heard speak of a knight in praise, but he caused him to be numbered of his household . . . Because of these noble lords about his hall, of whom each knight pained himself to be the hardiest champion, and none would count him the least praiseworthy, Arthur made the Round Table . . . It was ordained of Arthur that when his fair fellowship sat to meat, their chairs should be high alike, their service equal, and none before or after his comrade. Thus no man could boast that he was exalted above his fellow, for all alike were gathered round the board, and none was alien at the breaking of Arthur's bread.

Wace, Roman de Brut

A TABLE IN THE LIKENESS OF THE WORLD

Once the wars that attended Arthur's ascent to the throne were over, he decided to take a wife, and despite Merlin's warnings that she would one day betray him, he selected Guinevere, the daughter of King Leodegrance of Cameliarde. With her came, as dowry, a great round table, made by Merlin at the bidding of Arthur's father, Uther Pendragon. A table 'round in the likeness of the world', at which one hundred and fifty knights could sit, and none seem higher in favour than the rest. And on the day of his marriage, Arthur required of Merlin that he should find sufficient knights 'which be of most prowess and worship' to fill at least fifty of the seats.[47]

This Merlin did, and fifty more came from Leodegrance, so that a hundred sat down together at the table on that first day. And when they had all done homage to Arthur, they returned to the hall where the Round Table stood and found that on the back of each chair was a name, set there in golden letters. The names were all of those already chosen, and many more that were as yet not come. But two remained blank, and of these Merlin would only say enigmatically that they would be filled in due course.

ABOVE *Arthur's knights were sworn to fight against evil, right wrongs and redress injustice. Here Guerrehes rescues an old man from the clutches of armoured thugs.*

❖

❖

RIGHT *Sir Beaumains, the 'fair unknown' a young nobleman disguised as a humble boy, who rose to become one of Arthur's great knights.*

Thus the Fellowship of the Round Table met for the first time on the day of the king's wedding to Guinevere; and if the seeds were then already sown for the downfall of Arthur's great dream, the shadows were still distant on that day. For thus began the greatest ideal of chivalry ever to be known, the fame of which

THE
ELEMENT
LIBRARY
THE
ARTHURIAN
TRADITION

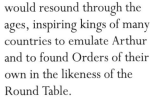

would resound through the ages, inspiring kings of many countries to emulate Arthur and to found Orders of their own in the likeness of the Round Table.

The knights' first adventure followed swiftly, for as they sat at dinner there came into the hall a white hart, pursued by a white dog and fifty couples of black hounds. As they raced around the Table, the white dog bit the hart which leapt high in the air, knocking over a knight who sat to one side. This man seized the dog and departed hurriedly. The next moment a lady rode into the hall and demanded that, the dog be brought back, for it was hers. But before anyone could answer, a fully armed knight rode among them, and

seizing the lady, carried her off by force.

Astonishment, and perhaps some amusement, attended these events. But Merlin stood forth and stated that the Fellowship 'might not leave these adventures so lightly'. So Arthur sent two of the new knights – his own nephew, Sir Gawain, and the illegitimate son of King Pellinore, Sir Tor – out after the white hart and the dog respectively; and Pellinore himself, a tried and trusted warrior, after the lady who had been stolen away.

So at the outset, this single incident had given rise to three separate adventures, which are there and then narrated at length. They are to be the first of many such adventures, which begin in similar fashion, with the entry of knight or lady into the court, requesting succour, or some favour of Arthur and of the Fellowship. Nor may the Round Table refuse, so long as the request is a fair one and the demand honest, for at the end of that first, triple quest, all of the Fellowship swears on oath:

❖❖

Never to do outrage nor murder, and always to flee treason; also, by no means to be cruel, but to give mercy unto him that asketh mercy, upon pain of forfeiture of their worship and lordship of King Arthur for evermore; and always to do ladies, damosels, and gentlewomen succour, upon pain of death. Also, that no man takes no battles in a wrongful quarrell for no law, nor for world's goods. Unto this were all the knights sworn of the table Round, both old and young. And every year were they sworn at the high feast of pentecost.[47]

❖❖

The rules are simply stated. They depend very much on the understood, but seldom phrased, ideals of medieval chivalry. Being human, not all of the knights keep to these demands placed upon them by their king. But despite some failings, they hold true to the honour of the Round Table, and as if in answer to their existence, strange events seem to multiply on every side, seeing to it that the knights never lack the opportunity of being tested and tried.

Arthur establishes a custom, at any high feast he will not eat until some wonder or adventure has been related to him. And so begins a pattern, whereby the knights ride 'at errantry', wandering hither and thither throughout the land in search of wrongs to right, or villainy to combat. Brother knights are rescued, as well as ladies; evil knights are overthrown and either killed or sent to Arthur to crave pardon. Many of these knights became Round Table Knights themselves, giving up their former pursuits. But there are always further adventures to attempt, as the great knights on their great horses thunder through the forests of Arthur's realm in quest of their King's dream of chivalry and the perfect earthly kingdom.

THE FOREST AND THE LANDS ADVENTUROUS

Most of the adventures of the Round Table Fellowship seem to take place in the setting of deep, primeval forest. This in part reflects the physical appearance of the countryside at the time when most of the romances were written; but there is a deeper significance than this. The forest symbolised an untamed world, where almost anything could, and did, lie in wait for the unwary. It stood, also, for a certain state of mind, a place to be reached on the long road from birth to death – Dante's impenetrable forest of the mind, in which the soul, wakening as he expressed it 'midway through life's journey', found itself with a thousand possible ways through the darkness of the world beneath the trees.[11]

The forest was part of the Otherworld, a vast uncharted tract which lay between the world of Middle Earth and the realms of Faery. Certain parts were given names: Broceliande, Arden, Inglewood: dark places redolent of enchantment, where only those intent upon adventure would willingly go. Here rode Arthur himself, in pursuit of innocent sport, to be met by the terrifyingly powerful Gromer Somer Joure, whose name means Man of the Summer's Day and who could bind Arthur at will and demand that he discover the answer to an impossible question, or face the consequences.[23]

On another occasion, while hunting, the Queen and her escort, who happened to be on this occasion Sir Gawain, became separated from the rest of their party and found themselves sheltering near the fearful Tarn Watheling, where more than one adventure had begun. There, they witnessed a horrific apparition, the ghost of Guinevere's mother

THE
ELEMENT
LIBRARY
THE
ARTHURIAN
TRADITION

who 'yammered' horribly at them and warned of dread things to come.

Yet though the forest contained many terrors, it contained as many wonders. From its depths appeared beautiful faery women, to test and beguile the wandering knights as they made their way through the trees. Many of these faery women sought husbands among the Fellowship who sired sons upon them – introducing a strain of Otherworldly blood into the company.

One such knight was Sir Launfal, who wandered into the Otherworld and met and married a beautiful fée. He was sworn to secrecy on pain of losing his love forever. Yet he was unable to keep silent when Queen Guinevere herself approached him with words of love, in desperation he declared that even she, for all her renowned beauty, was no match for his own dear love.

Earning in this way the enmity of the queen, Launfal faced death or banishment rather than speak further. He was finally vindicated by the appearance of the fée herself, who entered the court and outshone every woman there, and who then carried Launfal away with her, 'to Avalon, it is believed'.[48]

Not all such women encountered in the forest were as fair of face and speech. Ragnall, one of many archetypes of the sovereignty-bestowing goddess of the land, appeared as a hideous, 'Loathly Lady', who tricks Arthur into promising her the person of Sir Gawain in marriage in return for a favour. Her subsequent appearance at court, her gross manners and appearance, perhaps in part prepare one for her transformation, which occurs on the wedding night, when Ragnall, who has been 'enchanted', is restored to her true beauty through Gawain's love and understanding.

Elsewhere in the depths of the forest roamed the Questing Beast, a creature part lion, part serpent, part goat, which made a sound as though thirty couples of hounds were in its belly. Arthur first glimpses the Beast as a youth, before he is crowned king, and the sighting presages a meeting with Merlin.

ABOVE *The young Arthur encounters the elusive allegorical Questing Beast. King Pellinore, one of Arthur's allies, was doomed to spend his days in pursuit of this otherworldly chimera.*

❖

RIGHT *The Arthurian forest was peopled with enchanted beings who either ensnared the questing knights or helped them in their tasks.*

❖

Merlin appears first as a child, then as an old man who tells Arthur of his birth and parentage and makes many cryptic references to future events. The Beast does not explain, but we learn that it was borne by a woman who had condemned a man to be torn to pieces by dogs. It exists solely to be sought after, and is followed for many years by King Pellinore. After Pellinore's death, the Saracen knight Palomides takes up the quest but seems never to succeed, for this is a *ferlie*, a wonder out of the Otherworld which cannot be caught nor pinned down by any mortal being.

Men and women who had the power to change themselves into animals were not infrequent in the Arthurian world. In one story, Arthur follows a strange, composite beast which turns into a venerable white-haired man;[9] in another we have one of the earliest tales concerning a werewolf, *Bisclavret*,[48] in which a knight is cursed and is returned to his own form only after many years in wolf-shape.

In the Welsh story *The Lady of the Fountain*[46] we encounter 'the Lord of the Beasts', who

has one foot, one eye and one arm and who commands all the beasts of the forest who gather about him like a congregation listening to a sermon. When the knight Kynon asks him what power he has over the animals,

'I will show thee, little man, said he. And he took his club in his hand, and with it he struck a stag a blow so that he brayed vehemently, and at his braying the animals came together, as numerous as the stars in the sky... and he looked at them, and bade them go and feed; and they bowed their heads, and did him homage as vassals to their lord.[46]

Other knights become attached to a specific beast: Owain to a lion;[6] Gawain to a wondrous mule,[87] or a horse which leads him into strange lands.[59] These are all, to some extent, like the totem beasts of the shaman, which acts as guides to the soul in its journeys about the Otherworld. So many strange and wondrous beings emerge from the depths of the forest that one almost begins to wonder, after a time, if there is not some kind of

struggle going on between Arthur and the denizens of the Otherworld. An early Welsh poem, the *Preiddeu Annwn (Spoils of the Underworld)*, depicts him as leading an extraordinary band of heroes into the realm of the gods in search of a miraculous cauldron 'Warmed by the breath of Nine Maidens'. Passing through seven levels, each one guarded by a fortress – their names are Caer

ABOVE & LEFT
Animals appear in many forms in the Arthurian tradition as helpers, guardians and sometimes as adversaries, as above. In the story of Manus the grandson of the King of Orkney, a lion cub helped the hero to regain his inheritance as the King of Lochlann.

❖

THE
ELEMENT
LIBRARY
THE
ARTHURIAN
TRADITION

Siddi, Caer Rigor, Caer Vandwy, Caer Pedryfan, Caer Goludd, and Caer Ochren – Arthur and his men steal the cauldron and return with it to the outside world. 'Except seven, none returned', the poet remarks laconically, implying that the treasure was not brought out without cost.[45]

But the realms of faery and of Arthur overlap at every point. Even in the quest for the Grail, perhaps the greatest challenge to the Fellowship, the signs and symbols of the Otherworld are threaded like a strand of silver through the scarlet tapestry of Christian miracle and dream.

In the *Lais* of Marie de France,[48] composed in the twelfth century by this remarkable woman of whom virtually nothing is known, this Otherworldliness enters in as strongly as anywhere. Marie drew on tales then still circulating orally in France and Brittany – tales redolent with folklore and the magic of faery. Her stories are Celtic Wizardry in courtly dress, written for the elegant, literate audience at the court of another Marie, of Champagne, the daughter of the redoubtable

❖

BELOW *Dragons and damsels were constantly paired in the Arthurian world, a graphic representation of the pure and the profane.*

ABOVE *The slaying of monsters, giants and beasts was often an allegory for a successful fight against usurpers or invaders.*

❖

Eleanor of Aquitaine, who could herself have
passed for one of the gentlewomen of the
Arthurian milieu.

From the Lands Adventurous, via the Black
Pine, to the Fountain of Barenton, hidden
deep in the Valley of No Return, the Knights
of the Round Table rode 'overthwart and
endlong'[47] the length and breadth of the land.
Wherever the marvellous menagerie of their
heraldic devices – eagles, bulls, ravens and
lions – appeared, they were recognised, and
their aid or company sought. Like the
legendary 'fast guns' of the Old West, they
were sought out by those wishing to prove
themselves as the best among the chivalrons of
the land – maybe even earn themselves a seat
at the famous Table.

Two great families provided many of the
leading figures of the cycle: those of Orkney
and those of de Galles. The Orkney clan,
Gawain, Gaheries, Agravain and Gareth, were
the sons of King Lot of Orkney and his queen,
Morgause, who was Arthur's half-sister and
also the mother of the bastard Mordred. The
de Galles family, Perceval, Lamorack and
Aglovale, were the sons of King Pellinore (the
mother is not named) who also had numerous
illegitimate by-blows – including the great Sir
Tor or Torre – and a legitimate daughter who
is sometimes named Dindraine and who
played an important part in the Grail quest.

There was much rivalry between these two
families, sparked off by the killing of Lot by
Pellinore. After the killing, the Orkney

faction, led by Gawain, carried out several
murderous vengeance attacks which led to the
deaths of Morgause and Lamorack, who had
become lovers. Gaheries killed his own
mother and the brothers together slew
Lamorack.

Despite such internecine struggles, Malory
referred to the Fellowship as 'the high order
of Chivalry' and made of it something above
average for the time, more in line with the
ideal of chivalry expressed in treatises on the
subject, like that of the Spanish mystic Ramon
Lull[31] who saw chivalry as akin to priesthood,
with the 'Emperor' (i.e. the King – though
indeed in some texts Arthur does become
Emperor of Rome) taking a role similar to
that of the Pope as titular head of *all* knights.

THE
ELEMENT
LIBRARY
THE
ARTHURIAN
TRADITION

Rivalry between the Orkney clan and the de Galles family caused a great rift in the Fellowship of the Round Table.

❖

creation. They too sat at a round table and when Merlin brought the stones of the Giant's Dance from Ireland, to create what we now know as Stonehenge, he made that circle in the likeness of the Starry Table.

It does not matter that we know Merlin did not really build Stonehenge by magic, for we are speaking the symbolic language of myth, built layer upon layer in the consciousness of humanity. Thus, Merlin built his circular temple on the Table of the Earth, a third dimension which completes the parallels with the imagery of Robert de Borron, and may be expressed thus:

TRADITIONAL
Round Table of the Stars
Round Table of Arthur
Round Table of the Land

DE BORRON
Table of the Last Supper
Table of the Grail
Table of Arthur

Not only is there a hierarchical relationship established between the starry realms, the earthly kingship of Arthur, and the sacredness of the land; but there is also a direct relationship between the mystical opening up of the Christian message, the expression of this is in the Grail mysteries (see Chapter 6) and the Fellowship of the Round Table, who were destined to go in search of the sacred vessel.

Thus within the Arthurian tradition are inner realities expressed by outer symbolism. With the passing of the Fellowship on the terrible field of Camlan, nothing could be found to replace them. The country returned to the state of anarchy which had existed before the coming of Arthur. The Lands Adventurous faded from the minds of those who had once sought them out, and the Otherworld Forest was cut down. Yet the dream remained, as it does to this day. There are still those who would sit at the Round Table, to listen to the tales of the homecoming knights, and perhaps even brave an adventure or two themselves in the Otherworld realms of wonder.

The Round Table itself came to represent far more than a meeting place for the Fellowship. Robert de Borron,[43] tracking backward again as he had done in the story of Merlin, added a further dimension. The Table of Arthur, he declared, was made in the likeness of two earlier tables. The first, at which Christ and the Apostles sat to celebrate the Last Supper, had been copied by the Grail Kings as a suitable resting place for the Holy Cup itself, of which they were guardians and keepers. Finally, Merlin built the third table, at which the Fellowship would meet until the Grail itself appeared and sent them forth on the greatest quest of all, for which they had long been prepared.

Behind this idea lies another, subtler set of symbolic references. In the starry realms, according to many ancient traditions, met a council of mighty beings whose concern was with the execution of the divine plan of

4

GODDESSES
AND
GUIDES

Morgan Le Fay and the Otherworldly Women

Morgan le Fay, practises her necromantic arts.

❖

*T*hen fearlessly and unhesitatingly Geraint dashed forward into the mist. And on leaving the mist he
came into a large orchard; and in the orchard he saw an open space, wherein was a tent of red satin;
and the door of the tent was open, and an apple-tree stood in front of the door of the tent;
and on the branch of the apple-tree hung a huge hunting horn...And there was no-one in the tent
save one maiden sitting in a golden chair, and another chair was opposite to her, empty.
And Geraint went... and sat down therein.

Geraint, Son of Erbin from *The Mabinogion*

THE
ELEMENT
LIBRARY
THE
ARTHURIAN
TRADITION

GODDESSES WHO LEAD

The persona of Morgan le Fay threads through legend. Here she attends the birth of Ogier the Dane.

❖

There is a sense in which the majority of the women who appear in the Arthurian cycle are, or were, goddesses. That this is not immediately apparent is due to the gradual Christianisation of the material and to changing attitudes of successive storytellers, who altered, modified and sometimes suppressed many of the 'pagan' aspects of the tales they told.

Thus Morgan le Fay, whose origins have been traced to the Irish goddesses Macha and Morrighan, becomes in the medieval

Arthurian world, a mere enchantress — at least on the surface. Malory says of her that she was the daughter of Igrain and Gorlois of Cornwall, and that after her father's death and the events of Arthur's birth engineered by Merlin, she was 'put to school in a nunnery, where she became a great clerk of necromancy'.[47]

It is easy to see in this statement a reference to earlier times, when female children who displayed a talent for the second sight, or other aptitudes for the mystical life, were sent to be educated by schools of priestesses, such as once flourished in both Britain and Ireland. Morgan, who became known by the epithet 'le Fay', meaning the Fairy, retained some of her goddess-like qualities even in the medieval tales about her.

In Malory's work, while on the one hand she is portrayed as an enchantress and shape-shifter, Morgan also figures as one of the three mysterious queens who appear after the battle of Camlan to bear the wounded Arthur to Avalon, 'there to be healed of his wounds' and to await the time of his country's need.

Geoffrey of Monmouth, once again recording an ancient tradition, refers in his *Vita Merlini* to nine sisters who dwell on an island in the sea called 'the Fortunate Isle', or 'the Island of Apples'. He continues:

❦

She who is first of them is more skilled in the healing art, and excels her sisters in the beauty of her person. Morgan is her name, and she has learned what useful properties all the herbs contains, so that she can cure sick bodies. She also knows an art by which to change her shape, and to cleave the air on new wings like Daedalus.[21]

❦

Elsewhere in Malory, Morgan makes use of her shape-shifting ability by turning herself and her followers into rocks when they are pursued by Arthur and his knights.

Geoffrey's description of the wondrous island, with its sisterhood of nine, conforms in every detail to other accounts of the Celtic Otherworld. It is clear enough that Morgan is

LEFT *Sir Gawain fails in
his attempt to reach the
Grail. In the minds of
medieval chroniclers, his
complex and enigmatic
association with the
Goddess made him an
unsuitable candidate for
the Grail Quest.*

❖

the tutelary spirit, or goddess of this place,
and that her animosity towards Arthur (who
as her half-brother, has faery blood himself) is
merely an aspect of the challenging and testing
role which such figures eternally offer, in
order to discover who among their many
servants is truly worthy of favour.

Morgan appears again in this guise in the
marvellous Middle English poem *Sir Gawain
and the Green Knight,*[18] where she is the
organising principle behind the appearance of
the monstrous green giant at Camelot. The
story is typical of the role fulfilled by such
goddesses in Arthurian literature.

In the tale, which derives ultimately from an
ancient Irish source, Morgan's role is made to
seem slight by the poet, who sought a
Christian allegory in what was, essentially, a
pagan midwinter tale. (Yet even he called
Morgan 'the goddess', as did at least two
other medieval writers.)

I have dealt elsewhere with all of this in
some detail[59] and will say here only that it is
Morgan's presence which motivates the story,
which concerns nothing less than an initiation
designed specifically to test Gawain, and
through him the Round Table Fellowship, and
to prepare the hero for an even greater glory

LEFT *The Green Knight,
a creature of Morgan le
Fay, makes his dramatic
appearance at the court
of Camelot to frighten
Guinevere and to
challenge the honour and
integrity of Sir Gawain,
Arthur's nephew.*

❖

when he becomes the 'Knight of the
Goddess', her champion and lover in the
realms of men.

This initiatory sequence is continued and
completed in another poem of the same
period (thirteenth century), *The Wedding of Sir
Gawain and Dame Ragnall*[23] in which, as already
mentioned, Gawain is required to marry a

THE
ELEMENT
LIBRARY
THE
ARTHURIAN
TRADITION

hideously ugly hag, in order to save Arthur from death at the hands of the fearsome Gromer Somer Joure.

When, on their wedding night, Gawain suddenly finds that his hideous bride has become a ravishingly beautiful woman, he is given a further choice: to have her fair by night and foul by day, or vice versa. His response is to allow her to choose, and the spell is thus broken because Gawain gave her 'sovereignty', the right to be herself and to express her own nature – a rare enough thing in the repressive Middle Ages.

Behind this curious tale we catch a glimpse of an age-old theme, where the Goddess of Sovereignty herself encounters the new, young king of the land and by testing him proves his worthiness to rule. In the version outlined above, Gawain acts as Arthur's surrogate and is, at the same time, established as the Champion of the Goddess who through him offers her blessing upon the land.

Her choice of Gawain, Arthur's nephew, is not out of place. To the Celts, the relationship of sister's son was considered of equal or even greater worth than patrimony. It is more natural then, when Arthur begets a child with his half-sister Morgause. In the romances she is Morgan's sister, but it is easy to detect the presence of a single figure behind both – the Goddess of the Land, testing the young king. Mordred, the offspring of this union, becomes Arthur's nemesis – perhaps because, in his pride, Arthur refused to acknowledge the right, by Celtic law, of his sister's son to rule. (In the same way, he ordered the head of the god Bran the Blessed, buried under White Mount in London to offer protection against invasion, to be dug up, on the grounds that he alone should ward the land from its enemies.)

THE FLOWER BRIDE AND THE DARK GODDESS

between the champions of summer and winter for the hand of the Spring Maiden.

A version of this is told in *The Mabinogion* tale of Pwyll. Pwyll changes places for a year with Arawn, the Lord of the Otherworld, and undertakes one of Arawn's ritual tasks, an annual fight with Hafgan (Summer Song) for the possession of Creiddylad, the Maiden of Spring. We may judge the importance of this theme from the fact that as late as the nineteenth century, in Wales, teams of people led by a Lord of Summer and a Lord of Winter, were organised to engage in mock battle for the Maiden.

In the Arthurian tales, Lancelot, Guinevere's champion, becomes the bitter foe of Gawain, who is, as Knight of the Goddess, Morgan's champion. To begin with the two men are friends and this lasts through many adventures until Lancelot accidentally kills Gawain's brother.

It is one of the roles of the Flower Bride to be stolen away by one of her suitors and then to be rescued by another – thus forming an endless shifting of polarities with each succeeding seasonal change. In the case of Guinevere, we have a clear indication of her having fulfilled this role in a story contained in

ABOVE *The Dark Goddess, Morgan carried a branch from an apple tree, to signify her sovereignty of Avalon, the land of apples.*

❖

LEFT *When the Arthurian legends were reworked by Christian writers, both Guinevere, the goddess of flowers and light, and Morgan, the Dark Goddess, spent time in a nunnery.*

❖

FAR RIGHT *Guinevere at the stake as a punishment for her adultery. Mordred, Arthur's illegitimate son, had forced the king to punish the queen. She was rescued by her champion Lancelot.*

❖

In *Gawain and the Green Knight*, it is specifically stated that the reason why Morgan sent the Green Knight to Arthur's court was to frighten Guinevere. On one level, the reason for this was an old rivalry, dating from the time near the beginning of Arthur's reign when Guinevere had banished one of Morgan's lovers from court, thus beginning long-term hostilities. On another level, there is quite a different sort of rivalry between the two – that of two goddesses of very different aspect.

Morgan, as her origin in the savage figure of the Morrighan indicates, is a dark goddess, representing the powerful earthy qualities of winter and warfare. Guinevere, on the other hand, who was also once a goddess, is of the type called the Flower Bride, representing spring, the unfolding of life, the burgeoning of growth. As such, these two are in polarised opposition for all time. In the story of Guinevere's love for Lancelot, who becomes her champion and brings about the eventual ruin of the Round Table, it is even possible to see a pattern of the elemental struggle

THE
ELEMENT
LIBRARY
THE
ARTHURIAN
TRADITION

the *Life of Gildas* by Caradoc of Llancarfan.[7]

In this text, which deals with the deeds of a sixth-century saint who may actually have known the historical Arthur, we read how Melwas of the Summer Country carried off Guinevere, she had then to be rescued by Arthur – though not without the intervention of the saint. This story reappears in several versions within Arthurian literature, where the abductor had become Meliagraunce, a knight who desires Guinevere for his own. Then, the rescuer is Lancelot rather than Arthur, a seeming continuation of the various surrogate figures who stand in for the king at certain points in his life.

The identity of Melwas, or Meliagraunce, is not hard to fathom. In the *Life of Gildas* he is called King of the Summer Country – a name for the Otherworld. In the later versions, Meliagraunce is the son of King Bagdemagus

of Goirre or Gor, both names for the Otherworld. In the story of Pwyll, he is identified as Arawn, King of the Celtic Hades. Hence we have a scenario in which Guinevere is carried off into the Otherworld by its king or his representative, to be rescued by her champion. The Flower Bride is brought back in triumph to the court of her Lord, who is King of the Land.

We need only add that an earlier stage in the development of the Arthurian tradition, Gawain was the queen's champion. In the later texts he has changed allegiance from one aspect of the goddess to another, and has thus become the *opponent* of the Flower Bride's champion. This is, of course, a vastly simplified scenario; each aspect of the goddess has its own multifarious aspects – as we see from the sheer variety of roles fulfilled by the Otherworldly women in the Arthurian world.

THE INITIATORS

Lynette, the figure who comes to test Sir Gareth, actually appears as Lunete in another major story from the cycle, *Ywain* by Chrétien de Troyes. Here, she rescues the hero several times from death and gives him a ring which conveys the power of invisibility. A passage from Chrétien's poem makes her true identity clear:

I would like to make a brief mention of the friendship that was struck up in private between the moon and the sun. Do you know of whom I want to tell you? The man who was chief of the knights and honoured above them all should indeed be called the sun. I refer to my lord Gawain... And by the moon I mean she who is so uniquely endowed with good sense and courtly ways... her name is Lunete.[8]

ABOVE LEFT *Lanval, the hero of one of Marie de France's tales, was put to the test by a mysterious woman who forbade him to mention her, even when he was falsely accused of making advances to Guinevere.*

❖

LEFT *Morgan and three other faery queens find Lancelot vulnerable and sleeping in the forest.*

❖

So many initiators appear at Arthur's court, usually beginning as suppliants but ending as initiators, that it is not hard to perceive a clear pattern. Malory's 'Tale of Sir Gareth' from *Le Morte D'Arthur*,[47] is one of several stories which tell of 'The Fair Unknown'. Generally he is the son of a great hero who appears at court incognito, has various adventures, fights with his own brother or father and is finally recognised and honoured by all. In each of these stories, there is also a figure who performs the function of leading the hero through a series of adventures designed to test his skill and prowess. Almost without exception she possesses certain magical abilities and is active in arranging his eventual recognition.

ABOVE *In both Arthurian and folklore traditions there are a number of stories in which the hero, disguised as a kitchen boy, is subsequently discovered and acknowledged as a suitable candidate for knighthood.*

THE
ELEMENT
LIBRARY
THE
ARTHURIAN
TRADITION

The Tale of Sir Gareth
~

The hero, Gareth, is Gawain's youngest brother, the son of Morgause and Lot of Orkney. He chooses to remain incognito on his arrival at Arthur's court, and begs, as the first of three boons from the King, to be fed for a year. Kay, who takes charge of him, puts him in the kitchens and generally mocks him, naming him 'Beaumains', Fair Hands, because of his unusually large, white hands. Both Lancelot and Gawain befriend him that first year, though even the latter does not recognise his brother.

At the end of the year, a damsel named Lynette appears asking for a champion for her sister against Sir Ironside, the Red Knight of the Red Launds, who is besieging her castle. Gareth, alias Beaumains, now makes his two further requests: that he be given this adventure and that Lancelot should follow him and make him a knight when he deems the youth has earned it. Arthur agrees and Gareth and Lynette set out together, the maiden riding ahead and scorning anything to do with the 'kitchen knave' that King Arthur has seen fit to send with her.

During the succeeding days Gareth proves himself a sterling fighter and Lancelot, who has followed, declares Gareth a worthy opponent and knights him forthwith. Despite this, Lynette continues to upbraid her young escort, giving him a tongue-lashing at every opportunity. Gareth however, staunchly refuses to be drawn and performs ever more extraordinary deeds of prowess as he encounters a succession of knights in variously coloured armour – finally defeating the Red Knight of the Red Launds and winning the undying love of Lynette's sister, Lyonors.

The story does not end there, however. Lyonors bids her champion go forth to win even more honour before he

Gareth 'Beaumains' defeats
Sir Ironside the Red Knight
and wins the love of Lyonors.

❖

marries her. When he has gone, she changes her mind and requests her brother to lure him back again by pretending to kidnap a dwarf who has served him faithfully. All is reconciled and Gareth would have consummated his love before the wedding, had not Lynette prevented it by magical means. Lyonors holds a great tournament in which Gareth wears a magic ring enabling him to change the colour of his armour at will. He thus fights

several Round Table Knights incognito, then slips away unnoticed. Gawain sets out to discover the identity of the young knight and the two brothers meet and fight before Lynette arrives and stops them by identifying them to each other. She then heals their wounds with her magic and they return to the Court. Gareth is at last recognised as the son of Morgause and Lot and marries Lyonors at a splendid wedding feast.

Once again we recognise the figure of the goddess or Otherworldly woman who, once we have identified her, will be seen to appear in a hundred different guises throughout the Arthurian tradition. Her function is to guide and initiate tests and trials which bring about the transformation of the Round Table Fellowship from a simple chivalric order to a band of initiate knights. She it is who stands behind so much of the action and adventure in the stories – whether as Morgan le Fay, sending a magical cloak which consumes to ashes anyone who puts it on, or as Ragnall,

setting Gawain the supreme test of love. Such figures are an essential part of the inner dimension of the tradition. They are the initiators who cause things to happen, leaving the neophyte changed forever after. They are the polarised energy which drives the vast epic of Arthur from its dramatic beginnings to its climactic end. Without them the stories would be nothing more than a parade of meaningless images; with them they become a stately procession of wonders which open ever more doors, deeper into the enigmatic landscape of the Otherworld.

Gawain and the Green Knight
~

The Court is assembled for the Christmas feast, but before the feast can begin there is a crash of thunder and in through the door rides a monstrous figure wielding a mighty axe. He is green from head to foot: green skin, green clothes, green horse. Mocking the assembly he offers to play 'a Christmas game' with anyone who has the courage. The rules are as follows: that he will receive a blow with his own axe from any man there, on the understanding that he will give one back afterward. Gawain steps forward to accept the challenge. He strikes a single blow, severing the Green Knight's head from his body. But to everyone's horror, the giant picks up his head, holds it on high, and the lips move. He will expect Gawain in a year's time at the Green Chapel. Setting the head once more on his shoulders he departs as he came.

A year passes and Gawain prepares to set forth. He has no idea of the whereabouts of the Green Chapel and his wanderings take him into the Wilderness of Wirrall, where he faces danger from trolls and the harsh winter weather. Half dead from cold and fatigue, he arrives at the castle of Sir Bercilak, a larger-than-life figure who offers him hospitality and introduces him to his beautiful wife, who is accompanied by a hideous old woman. Bercilak declares that he knows where the Green Chapel is, a mere few hours' ride away, and declares his intention of going hunting. When Gawain declines to accompany his host, preferring to rest, Bercilak proposes a sporting exchange of winnings: he will give Gawain whatever spoil he derives from the day's hunting, in exchange for anything his guest has won during the same period.

Once Bercilak has departed, his wife enters Gawain's room and does her best to seduce him. Gawain politely refuses but is forced to accept a single kiss. When Bercilak returns with the spoils of the hunt, all that Gawain has to exchange is the kiss. The same thing happens on the next two days, the lady of the castle amorously approaching her guest and Gawain accepting first two, then three kisses, which he duly exchanges with his host. On the fourth day Gawain confesses his errand and says that he has little chance of surviving. Lady Bercilak offers him a green baldric which protects its wearer from all harm. This Gawain accepts, with some hesitation, and does not declare it in his day's 'winnings'.

Next morning Gawain sets out for the Green Chapel, and on arrival finds the Green Knight busy sharpening his axe. Gawain kneels in the snow and his adversary twice feints, until Gawain is angered and bids him strike once and for all. The third blow of the axe merely nicks Gawain's neck, at which he leaps up, declaring honour satisfied and calling on the Green Knight to defend himself. Whereat the giant laughs long and loud saying that the 'game' is over. He goes on to admit that he is really Sir Bercilak, enchanted into his present shape by the arts of 'Morgane the goddess', who is really the old crone at the castle. Gawain has come through with honour unstained, except for accepting the green baldric from Lady Bercilak, for which reason he received the nick from the Green Knight's axe. Gawain returns to Camelot and tells his story. All the knights decide to wear green sashes to honour Gawain's successful adventure.

5

LANCELOT
AND
TRISTAN

True Love and Perfect Chivalry

Ah! he wanders forth again;
We cannot keep him; now, as then,
There's a secret in his breast
Which will never let him rest.

Tennyson, Idylls of the Kings

LOVE'S DANCE

There is a great deal about love in the Arthurian cycles, ranging from the openly sensual (what a seventeenth-century Puritan referred to as 'bold bawdy') to the deeply mystical. Treatment of the character of Gawain, who began life as a heroic figure dedicated to the service of the feminine principle (the goddess), and ended it as a libertine, exemplifies the way in which shifting cultural forces changed the way successive generations of writers chose to depict love.

To the Celts love was a joyful sport in which all men and women engaged as a matter of course. Sex itself was frequently depicted as a way of reaching a mystical relationship with the elements hence the idea of Sacred Kingship and the marriage with the land; while countless meetings with Maidens of the Wells engendered heroes who were more than half of the Otherworld. Many of the premier heroes of the Arthurian cycles originated in this way, including Arthur himself, Gawain and both the great heroes dealt with in this chapter.

Indeed, if one is looking for proof of the Celtic origins of the Arthurian tradition, one

OPPOSITE *Troubadours from southern France celebrated the ideal of Courtly Love embodied by the relationship between Lancelot and Guinevere and Tristan and Isolt.*

❖

ABOVE *The infant Lancelot is snatched away by the Lady of the Lake.*

❖

LEFT *Lancelot and Tristan, fellow Knights of the Round Table. They were well matched in battle and became friends after they had fought each other.*

❖

THE
ELEMENT
LIBRARY
THE
ARTHURIAN
TRADITION

need look no further than the often complex love-lives of these two heroes – despite the fact that by the time the full glory of the literary heritage occurred, during the Middle Ages, love had begun to be seen in a very different way. Sometimes love as a cult occupation with all the trappings of religion, sometimes as a sinful pastime best expunged from the human system, and sometimes as a romantic experience which foreshadows the ideas of the eighteenth and nineteenth centuries.

Lancelot's literary origins are more vague than those of Tristan. Lancelot almost certainly derives from a character named Llwch Lleminiawg, who appears by name in *the Mabinogion* and in the poem *The Spoils of Annwn* already referred to. He carries a fiery sword and may thus be seen as a type of solar hero like Gawain, with whom he shares several other attributes. Apart from these few sparse references, nothing more is known of him until he reappears in a twelfth-century Swiss poem called *Lanzalet*,[37] but here he has yet to acquire his best-known role as Guinevere's lover.

Lanzalet is almost certainly based on a lost Celtic original which must have told more of the early history of the hero, but for the rest we have to make recourse to medieval texts for a fuller account.

❖

BELOW *Lancelot du Lac was an established hero in the French versions of the Arthurian tradition. Here he is shown with the king and other knights in a Medieval French illustrated manuscript.*

For Tristan, on the other hand, we have a more detailed set of references. He may, indeed, have been a genuine historical personage, Drust or Drustan, son of Talorc or Tallwch. Evidence suggests that he was of Pictish origin, which possibly makes him older than any of the Arthurian heroes, since the Picts were an indigenous population in Britain before the coming of the Iberian Celts. Fragmentary references to his story, which involves his liaison with the wife of March ap Meirchawn (the King Mark of later stories), are found scattered throughout Celtic literature. In the *Triads*[6] he is referred to as one of the 'Three Mighty Swineherds of the Island of Britain', who guarded the swine of March ap Meirchawn, while the swineherd went to ask Esyllt to come to meet with him'.

Here we have a clear reference to the traditional triangular relationship between Tristan, Isolt and Mark. The association of Tristan with pigs, sacred to the Celtic Mother Goddess, is also noteworthy. Where the outward story of love and betrayal exists, there is a shadowy underpinning of Otherworldly characters who reflect and influence the lives of the mortals in the outside world. If we look more closely at the histories of the two heroes, we will see how this Otherworldly influence reveals itself at almost every point in their lives.

THE ILL-MADE KNIGHT

On the face of it, there is little essential difference between the stories of Lancelot and Tristan. Both are born and raised away from their original homes and families; both are mighty fighters, unequalled in their time; both are considered exemplars of courtly love, the sophisticated and elaborate code devised by the twelfth-century troubadours which made a virtue of love outside the bonds of marriage, and raised the service of lover to beloved to an almost religious ritual.

Yet there are differences, which became apparent when one examines their lives in greater detail. It is a difference, ultimately, between kinds of love, which each man in his way represents.

Lancelot is the son of King Ban of Benwick and his queen, Elaine. Shortly after their son's birth, Ban, who is one of the staunchest supporters of the young Arthur in the early days of his reign, becomes involved in a war with the neighbouring king, Claudas. Claudas

*Sir Lancelot, the greatest
knight at Arthur's court
in his prime.*

❖

eventually overruns Ban's lands and forces the
rightful king and queen to flee. As they are
escaping, Ban looks back to see his home in
flames and the sight causes him to fall in a
swoon from which he never rises. His queen,
hurrying to his aid, leaves their son who is
then named Galahad, unattended for a
moment only. In that time the Lady of the
Lake appears and steals the child away to her
palace beneath the waters. Heartbroken,
Queen Elaine builds a church on the site of
the hill where King Ban fell. The infant
Galahad, now renamed Lancelot of the Lake,
grows to manhood in the company of women
and the faery-like mermen of the lady's
palace. He learns quickly and develops great
strength and skill in arms. He meets his
cousins, Bors and Lional, and a half-brother
named Ector, and when Lancelot reaches the
age of eighteen, the four young men set out
for Arthur's court and the famous Fellowship
of the Round Table.

In memory of King Ban's support during his
youth, Arthur heaps favours on the
newcomer, dubbing Lancelot a knight on St
John's Day. In some versions of the story, one
of Lancelot's first tasks is to fetch Arthur's
bride, Guinevere the daughter of King
Leodegraunce, to Camelot for her wedding,
and on this occasion she and Lancelot first
begin to fall in love. In other texts, Guinevere
is already established when Lancelot arrives,
and he soon becomes one of the Queen's
Knights, a kind of sub-order of the Round
Table to which young and aspiring knights
were attached before they had fully proved
themselves. Lancelot then begins a whole
series of adventures which establish him,
beyond question, as the greatest knight of his
time. Among other deeds, he conquers the
dark custom of a castle named Dolorous
Gard, which then becomes his own home and
is renamed Joyous Gard. In the haunted
graveyard of the castle, Lancelot raises the lid
of a great tomb which no-one else can move.
He finds written within his true name and
lineage and a prophecy regarding his own son,
whose name will also be Galahad.

Returning to Camelot Lancelot becomes a
Knight of the Round Table. He aids Arthur in
putting down the rebellion of Galehaut the
Haut Prince, who surrenders to Arthur after

THE
ELEMENT
LIBRARY
THE
ARTHURIAN
TRADITION

Lancelot and Elaine of Astolat. She was the first lady for whom he was champion; he accepted her favour to wear in his quest and gave her his shield in exchange. She fell in love with him, but he did not return her feelings and she died of a broken heart.

observing Lancelot's chivalry and fortitude in battle. Galehaut afterwards becomes Lancelot's closest friend and in an episode later made famous by Dante[11] acts as a confidential go-between for the tongue-tied knight and the queen.

There follows the episode the False Guinevere (see Chapter 1) during which time the real queen takes refuge with Lancelot in Galehaut's kingdom of Surluse (possibly the Scilly Isles). After the discovery and death of the False Guinevere, Lancelot restores the real queen to Arthur. But by this time Lancelot and Guinevere are irrevocably in love, and Lancelot's life becomes an endless struggle with his conscience which leads him to pursue quest after quest in order to be away from the court and the queen. On one such adventure he rescues a lady from a bath of boiling water in which she has been imprisoned by enchantment for several years. This is Elaine of Corbenic, daughter of King Pelles the Grail

Guardian, and by means of a trick Lancelot is persuaded that he is visiting Guinevere. He engenders upon Elaine the son who is to be named Galahad and who will grow up to be the destined Grail winner. P. L. Travers has suggested that Lancelot may have taken a vow of celibacy when he could not love Guinevere. The knowledge that he had not only betrayed his love for Guinevere but had broken this vow drove Lancelot mad for a time. He is eventually discovered wandering naked and starving in the forest and nursed back to health by Elaine, with whom he returned to Joyous Gard for a time.

Soon after this begins the quest for the Grail, which will be dealt with more fully in the next chapter. Lancelot's part in this is ambiguous. The coming of his son Galahad sets the whole adventure in motion, and the two, father and son, establish a deep relationship which is, however, to be short-lived since Galahad dies at the end of the quest. Lancelot himself has several visions of the Grail, and finally comes to the very door of the chapel where the holy vessel is kept. But he is prevented from entering by an angelic presence and falls into a trance which lasts for several weeks. It is made clear to Lancelot, before the quest is at an end, that his failure is due solely to his love for the queen, which exceeds his love for God, and for a time he is determined to renounce it. But, once the Grail quest is over Lancelot resumes his old habits, and the seal is set upon the downfall of the Arthurian dream.

After the quest, with many of the older knights dead or lost, a younger contingent comes to the fore, and Mordred, Arthur's illegitimate son, begins to plot the destruction of the Fellowship. Capturing Lancelot and Guinevere in the queen's chamber, just when they had reached a decision to end their long association for the good of the kingdom, Mordred forces Arthur to condemn his queen to the stake. Lancelot rescues her, but in the process accidentally kills Gareth and Gaheris, Gawain's brothers. Thus a war is initiated which is wished for by neither party but which ends in the death of Gawain and news that Mordred, left in charge of the kingdom

ABOVE *Lancelot is refused sight of the Grail, due to his misdemeanours with Guinevere*

❖

while Arthur pursued Lancelot to his homeland in France, has declared his father dead and himself king. Returning, Arthur fights a last battle against his son and receives the wound which sends him to Avalon. Lancelot, hearing of all this, comes too late to the aid of his old friend. He visits Guinevere, now in a nunnery at Amesbury, one last time, and having taken leave of her puts aside his knightly weapons and armour to adopt the life of a hermit. As such he lives out his last days, finally hearing of Guinevere's death and not long outliving her. He is taken to be buried at Joyous Gard, while Guinevere is laid to rest beside Arthur. Lancelot's half-brother, Sir Ector, almost the last of the original

Fellowship to survive, delivers the following eulogy, which could be said to speak for all the knights:

◆⟍⟋

Ah Lancelot, thou are head of all Christian knights, and now I dare say, thou Sir Lancelot, there thou liest, that thou was never matched of earthly knights. And thou were the courteous knight that ever bare shield. And thou were the truest friend to thy lover that ever bestrad horse. And thou were the truest lover of a sinful man that ever loved woman. And thou were the kindest man that ever struck with sword. And thou were the goodliest person that ever came among press of knights. And thou was the meekest man and the gentlest that ever ate in hall among ladies. And thou were the sternest knight to thy mortal foe that ever put spear in the rest.[47]

⟍⟋◆

Thus ends the story of the greatest of all Arthurian knights, and perhaps, the most tragic. Lancelot is caught between the pull of love and duty and in the struggle to maintain both, perishes, bringing down the kingdom with him. His failure in the Grail quest is one of the most painful stories in the entire cycle; so great is Lancelot's heart that he comes as

RIGHT *Lancelot, the 'ill-made knight', in the chamber of Queen Guinevere. Their relationship destroyed Arthur's kingdom and prevented Lancelot from attaining the Grail.*

❖

THE
ELEMENT
LIBRARY
THE
ARTHURIAN
TRADITION

near as any to achieving this most central of
adventures. Yet he is not strong enough, and
his failure is greater because it was almost
success. His love for Guinevere proves
stronger than his love for God, but it is a pure
love in its fashion. Over the many years of his
single-minded devotion to the woman he
loves, Lancelot never so much as looks at
another (with the exception of Elaine, who
tricks him into her bed). When he hurries to
win her back from Meleagraunce, he rides
almost without hesitation in a cart – a vehicle

reserved in those day for criminals, the dead
or the transportation of dung – only to be
condemned by Guinevere on arrival for having
hesitated even as much as a second. Yet in the
face of this and other occasions when the
queen doubts his faithfulness, he remains
staunch in his love.

These very human characteristics make
Lancelot one of the most unforgettable people
in the entire cycle, from whom much can be
learned by those who seek to understand the
importance of the Arthurian tradition.

THE SAD ONE

*As a rather hot-headed
young squire, Tristan
killed his proud and
discourteous master Sir
Calidon and became a
knight himself.*

❖

Tristan's story, though outwardly similar to
Lancelot's, is at heart very different. The son
of King Meliodas and Queen Elisabeth of
Lyonesse, he acquires his name (derived from
the French *triste,* meaning sorrow) from the
circumstances of his birth. His father having
been stolen away by an enchantress, his

mother, though heavy with child, goes in
search of her husband. She gives birth to her
son in the depths of the forest, where she soon
dies. Thereafter, Tristan is brought up by a
vassal of King Meliodas named Governal, until
his step-mother tries to poison him so that her
own sons may inherit. After this attempt on
his life, he is sent abroad in the care of
Governal, where he is schooled in the courtly
arts of hunting and hawking, and becomes an
especially skilled harpist.

After a few years, Tristan returns to Britain
and visits the court of his uncle, King Mark of
Cornwall. There he learns of an annual
tribute paid by youths and maidens to the
King of Ireland. He agrees to act as King
Mark's champion and fights the gigantic Irish
warrior known as the Morold on an island in
the sea. He is victorious and slays the Morold,
but in so doing receives a poisoned wound.
The wound refuses all treatment and soon
begins to smell so badly that, on the advice of
a wise woman, Tristan is set adrift in a small
boat, in which manner he reaches Ireland.
There he is taken to the daughter of the Irish
king, who is named Isolt, and who is much
skilled in healing. Calling himself 'Tantrist'
and passing himself off as an itinerant harpist,
Tristan is almost killed when Isolt discovers
the real identity of her patient. The Morold
was her uncle and she has to be restrained
from turning upon his slayer; but as the weeks
pass her hatred turns to liking and then love.

The couple exchange rings before Tristan leaves Ireland to return to Mark's court, but once there he seems to forget Isolt because we next hear of him in rivalry with Mark for the favours of the wife of Segwarides. Perhaps because of this Mark turns against his young nephew, and when pressure from his barons forces the king to look for a wife, he sends Tristan across to Ireland to seal the uneasy peace between the two countries by requesting the hand of Isolt of Ireland. Tristan has no difficulty in arranging this, since he had struck up a lasting friendship with Isolt's father King Anguish. But on the voyage home the couple inadvertently drink a love potion, which had been prepared by Isolt's mother and was intended to ensure the success of Isolt's wedding with Mark. Tristan and Isolt become lovers in earnest.

Brangane, Isolt's faithful servant, sacrifices her own virginity by pretending to be her

LEFT *In one version of the story, Tristan leaps from a high window to escape imprisonment and return to his love Isolt.*

❖

❖

BELOW *Brangane, Isolt's servant comforts her mistress. After his banishment from the court of King Mark, Tristan disguised himself as a beggar to visit the queen secretly, but was recognised by her brachet hound.*

mistress on the wedding night. Tristan and Isolt, now Isolt of Cornwall, meet on any and every occasion, devising an intricate system for passing messages. They continue to cuckold Mark for a number of years, until a jealous knight named Andret

LEFT *The doomed lovers Tristan and Isolt meet in secret at every opportunity. Their obsessive enchantment with each other characterised the negative aspects of Courtly Love.*

❖

THE
ELEMENT
LIBRARY
THE
ARTHURIAN
TRADITION

gives them away and they are forced to flee. Taking up a wandering, idyllic life in the depth of the forest of Morrois, they are eventually discovered by Mark, who on seeing them sleeping with a sword between them (an accident rather than an intentional act) believes that he may have wronged the couple and offers to take Isolt back on condition that Tristan goes into exile.

Wandering into Britain, the hero becomes a Knight of the Round Table and soon proves himself equal to the very best of the Fellowship, at one time fighting even Lancelot to a standstill – though the contest remains inconclusive. The two become friends, but Tristan is soon driven to wander again, and in Brittany he takes service with King Hoel, whose daughter also happens to be called Isolt – Isolt of Brittany. Tristan becomes friends with her brother who persuades him to marry this second Isolt; but the marriage is never consummated and shortly afterwards Tristan returns to Cornwall and steals the first Isolt

away. They find refuge for a time in Lancelot's castle of Joyous Gard, until Arthur intervenes to persuade Mark to forgive them both and to take Isolt back once again. Returning to Brittany, Tristan is wounded in a battle in which he fights on the side of King Hoel. He sends word to Isolt of Cornwall to come and heal him. To the sailors who take this message he gives instruction that if they are successful they are to display a white sail, but that if Isolt refuses to come, they should show a black sail. Isolt comes indeed, but her namesake, who loves Tristan deeply and is jealous of his great passion, tells him the sail is black. Whereat Tristan turns his face to the wall and dies. Isolt of Cornwall, arriving to find her lover dead, lies down beside him and herself expires. They are buried in adjoining graves from which spring forth red and white briars, which twine together in token of a love that reaches beyond death. Isolt of Brittany throws herself from a cliff and dies; Mark lives on to ravage Arthur's lands after the king's death.[3]

Brittany, Tristan's place of exile after he was expelled from the court of King Mark in Cornwall. Here, the young knight served King Hoel and married his daughter, Isolt of Brittany. It was from such a cliff that Isolt cast herself in despair after Tristan's death.

❖

THE TWO FACES OF LOVE

Tristan, 'the sad one', and Lancelot, 'the ill-made knight', span the entire gamut of passionate relationships, yet their stories, though essentially alike, are different in kind. Lancelot is essentially a man of honour, whose very real pain at the betrayal of the king he loves and serves makes him the most human of the characters in the cycle. From the very beginning, once he has recognised the love which he shares with Guinevere, he loses no opportunity to be away from the court – becoming, with each successive adventure, both more honoured and more desirable to women. Yet despite himself he is helpless, returning again and again to the queen like a falcon to the lure.

Tristan, on the other hand, is a more amoral figure altogether. We see him wooing Isolt of Ireland and then the next moment chasing the wife of Sir Segwarides. Later, after long years as Isolt of Cornwall's lover, he is persuaded to marry her namesake of Brittany. Nor is he averse to playing all kinds of tricks upon Mark, including dressing as a beggar and carrying Isolt across a stream so that she can swear a public oath that no-one else had ever laid a finger upon her.

Then there is the matter of the love potion, intended for Isolt and Mark. Much has been written about this and the effect it has upon the 'morality' of the tale. It is quite clearly part of the earliest version of the story, and though some texts indicate that its efficacy was only for a period of five years, it is an essential part of the scenario. The question is whether it is the cause of the love between Tristan and Isolt, or whether their passion would have come about in spite of it. There can be no real answer to this; we can only look at the story as we have it and judge for ourselves. A later text, the *Tavola Ritonda* (Round Table)[69] reports that Pope Agapitas (*sic*) granted indulgences to all who prayed for the souls of Tristan and Isolt, since it was the work of the potion which caused them to fall into sin! Another aspect of the story which casts a different light upon Tristan's role is the character of Mark. Unlike Arthur, he is very far from a noble king, being not above giving Isolt to a band of lepers as a punishment for her betrayal of the marriage vows. He several times plans to have Tristan killed, and in at

LEFT *Tristan and Isolt of Ireland drank the love potion in ignorance. Therefore their adulterous obsession may be seen as a force outside them, something beyond their control.*

❖

LEFT *Lancelot's lifetime passion for Queen Guinevere is made even more poignant, hopeless and human because he also loved Arthur, and was sworn to protect and defend him. Here he stays the hand of Sir Bors, who is about to kill the king, even though Arthur's death would free Guinevere.*

❖

THE
ELEMENT
LIBRARY
THE
ARTHURIAN
TRADITION

least one version of the story is successful.[47] But what can we learn from all of this, aside from the obvious moral lesson? How does the love of Lancelot for Guinevere, of Tristan for Isolt, fit in with the idea of chivalry? Malory, in a great and justly famous passage, makes the following observation:

❧

Like as winter rasure doth always arase and deface green summer, so fareth it by unstable love in man and woman. For in many persons there is no stability; for we may see all day, for a little blast of winter's rasure, anon we shall deface and lay apart true love for little or naught, that cost much thing... But the old love was not so; men and women could love together seven years... and then was love, truth and faithfulness: and lo, in like wise was used love in King Arthur's days.

(Le Morte D'Arthur Bk XVII, Ch.25.)

❧

The faithfulness of lover to beloved seems more important here than that of husband to wife, and indeed so it was held by a majority of people in a time when marriages were arranged for political reasons rather than for love. The teaching of the troubadours, who wandered through most of Europe during the time when the Arthurian tradition was at its height, are to be felt in almost every part of the stories of Lancelot and Tristan. For the troubadours, love was impossible between married people, and they placed the figure of the beloved on a pedestal, from which it was not to be dislodged until the reactionary backlash of the seventeenth-century Puritan ethic. So strong became Courtly Love that the Church was forced to declaim against it. This too can be felt within the Arthurian canon, where a new kind of love, as portrayed by the quest for the Holy Grail, began to change the shape of the stories.

A CERTAIN INBORN SUFFERING

Courtly Love, the 12th-century code of chivalric convention between the sexes endowed each partner with the equal rights to power and passion.

❖

In the twelfth century, when Courtly Love was at its height, a clerk in the service of Marie de Champagne, daughter of the great Queen Eleanor of Aquitaine, composed a book of rules which codified the conventions governing the lover's every act. He called it *The Art of Courtly Love*[1] and in it he gave a very different definition to that which Malory was to give nearly three hundred years later.

❧

Love is a certain inborn suffering derived from the sight of and excessive meditation on the beauty of the opposite sex, which causes each one to wish above all things the embraces of the other and by common desire to carry out all of love's precept in the other's embrace.[47]

❧

This certainly describes the intensity of passion evinced by both the great heroes and their queenly loves, though it fails to plumb

the mystery which fuelled both. A quotation, from the greatest medieval retelling of the Tristan story, by Gottfried von Strassbourg,[22] gives yet another dimension to it all.

In the story, the lovers have escaped and found refuge in the forest of Morrois where they live an idyllic life together. Embroidering on the original version, Gottfried describes them as inhabiting a fantastic cave which he describes in intricate detail:

❧

This grotto was round, high, and perpendicular, snow-white, smooth, and even, throughout its whole circumference. Above, its vault was finely keyed, and on the keystone there was a crown most beautifully adorned with goldsmiths' work and encrusted with precious stones. Below, the pavement was of smooth, rich, shining marble, as green as grass. At the centre was a bed most perfectly cut from a slab of crystal... dedicated to the Goddess of Love. In the upper part of the grotto some small windows had been hewn out to let in the light, and through these the sun shone in several places.[22]

❧

Gottfried interprets this fantastic place for us. It is round, broad, high and perpendicular and a token of love's simplicity and power and love's aspiration which 'mounts aloft to the clouds'. The crown stands for the virtues of love, while the bed is of crystal in token of the transparency and translucency of all true love. Even the windows stand for 'Kindness… Humility…and Breeding', through which the light of honour shines.

Here then, love is still honour, even though the world would see it otherwise. Love is also joy and offers an example which can transform others. As Gottfried says:

If the two of whom this love-story tells had not endured sorrow for the sake of joy, love's pain for its ecstasy within one heart, their name and history would never have brought such rapture to so many noble spirits.[22]

In the end then, human passion becomes inspiration. We may even see behind this a deeper message, leading back to the simpler times in which stories were born. According to this way of seeing things, the human lovers are surrogates who allow the gods themselves to experience love in its every aspect. Through this love, the gods are better able to know the ways of mortals and to strengthen the interaction between the worlds, keeping open the channels that mediate between the human and the divine.

Significantly, both Lancelot and Tristan love queens. Here in a passage from the *Perceval* of Chrétien de Troyes, Gawain refers to Guinevere:

Just as the wise master teaches young children, my lady the queen teaches and instructs every living being. From her flows all the good in the world, she is its source and origin. Nobody can take leave of her and go away disheartened, for she knows what each person wants and the way to please each according to his desires.[49]

Much within the stories of Lancelot and Tristan becomes clear. What all the troubadours and their ilk were saying in every song and poem they wrote was that it is the

divine element within all women which serves to fuel and inspire men to heights beyond their normal reach. Thus chivalry itself is informed by love, just as love is informed by the service required by all who take the vows of chivalry seriously. Love itself thus becomes an initiation, which is why we find so many of the women who feature within the Arthurian cycles to be of Otherworldly stock. We have seen that many of the heroes who court or worship, or even marry them, share this heritage also. In the end, the worlds are brought together at every level, physical, emotional and spiritual. The spiritual world, represented by the quest for the Grail, shows another face of love.

Unrequited love had its place in the Courtly Love convention. The Lady of Shalot in Tennyson's poem (possibly Elaine of Astolat) suffered and died from her unreciprocated feelings for Lancelot.

6

THE
GRAIL QUEST

*Spirituality and the
Search for Absolutes*

*W*hen they were all seated and the noise was hushed, there came a clap of thunder so loud and
terrible that they thought the palace must fall. Suddenly the hall was lit by a sunbeam
which shed a radiance through the palace seven times brighter than had been before...
When they had sat a long while thus, unable to speak and gazing at one another like dumb animals, the
Holy Grail appeared, covered with a cloth of white samite; and yet no mortal hand was seen to bear it.
It entered through the great door, and at once the palace was filled with fragrance as though all the
spices of the earth had been spilled abroad.

Queste del Saint Graal

THE CAULDRON OR THE CUP

As the great visionary Dion Fortune wrote, almost fifty years ago, 'There are times in the history of races when the things of the inner life come to the surface and find expression, and from these rendings of the veil the light of the sanctuary pours forth.'[15]

Thus it was with the legends of the Grail. Too long ago now to identify with any degree of certainty, an idea found crystallisation in the form of a sacred vessel which contained the potentiality of all wisdom and knowledge, and through them of understanding. In ancient Hellenic mystery teachings it was the *Crater*, the Cup in which the gods mixed the very stuff of creation. The Sufis saw it as the Cup of Jamshid, from which knowledge and divine inspiration were dispensed. Its image is found in India, in Japan, in the Russias, and among the Celtic peoples, where it is recognised as the life-bestowing Cauldron belonging to the Goddess Ceridwen or the God Bran.

Sometime near the beginning of the eleventh century, perhaps influenced by the inner, magical history of the time, someone wrote a story which clothed either a Celtic or an Oriental tale in the dress and manners of the time. We do not know the identity of this writer, though tradition gives him a name at

least – Blihis or Bliheris – singular among the writers of the Arthurian tradition for appearing as a *character* in a later text.[14] Whether he spoke of a Cauldron or a Cup we cannot know, since all traces of that story have vanished. Nor is it perhaps necessary to know which it was – or for that matter which influenced the other. Much controversy has raged over the nature and appearance of the Grail, whether it is a pagan symbol or a Christian image. But in the end such speculations are fruitless, taking one away from the essential meaning of the story rather than further into it. There are, indeed, aspects of the Grail which seem to reflect the wonder-working Cauldron; and there is that about the Cauldron, which seems to prefigure the medieval accounts of the Grail. Whatever the truth, it is in these later, generally Christian versions of the story, that its true power is revealed.

THE
ELEMENT
LIBRARY
THE
ARTHURIAN
TRADITION

THE PERFECT FOOL

ABOVE *Joseph of Arimethea, who was believed to have been given the Grail by the risen Christ and to have brought it to Britain.*

❖

The first written story of the Grail which is still extant makes it neither pagan or Christian – though we can interpret it either way.

About 1180, Chrétien de Troyes, already famous for his poems on various aspects of the Arthurian tradition, began work on his final romance, *Perceval, of the Story of the Grail*.[8] He died before finishing it, and left an enigma which has exercised the minds and haunted the dreams of countless seekers after wisdom ever since. The story tells us of Perceval's discovery of the Grail but then turns to the

adventures of Gawain, who is in search of the Grail. Halfway through this part of the story the narrative breaks off in mid-sentence, leaving everything unexplained.

So great was the power of this mystery that no less than four other writers attempted, with varying degrees of success to complete Chrétien's story. Long before they did so, however, other, possibly independent versions appeared. We have already seen how Robert de Borron wrote a trilogy of works in which he attempted to fill in the missing parts of the story. In doing so he made the identification of the Graal or Grail with the Cup of the Last Supper, and thus made the story for all time part of Christian tradition. That he may not have been the first to do so is not important (he makes the statement that he is following another text); it is his version of the story that is remembered, and which probably sparked off a succession of further narratives in which the story of the Grail reached a level of detail and power probably undreamed of by either Chrétien or Robert – and most certainly by the mysterious Blihis.

Perceval, the 'Perfect Fool', was established as the champion of the Grail, and several stories of increasing complexity extended his role and attempted to explain the meaning of the Grail in bewildering detail. New dimensions were added at every point. The

RIGHT *The plain cups and bowls used by Christ and his disciples at the Last Supper also inspired the Grail legend.*

❖

LEFT *The Procession of
the Sangrail at Grail
castle as witnessed by
Perceval, according to
Chrétien de Troyes in*
Perceval. *The Holy
Grail was hidden and
protected at all times;
only a few might see it
and only one could
become the
Grail Knight.*
❖

Grail Guardian became one of a family of such people, descended from Joseph of Arimathaea, the rich Jew who gave up his own tomb to house the body of Christ and was said to have received the Grail – and its secret teachings – from the risen Messiah.

Somewhere along the way someone explained the reason for the ancient king's infirmity by declaring him the victim of a blow struck, either accidentally or as the retribution for some great wickedness, by the knight Balin the Savage – seen by some as a representative of paganism. This became known as the Dolorous Blow, and not only did it cause an unhealing wound which could only be set right by the destined Grail winner, but also laid waste the Kingdom of the Grail Family, which became a desert place in which the most terrible adventures and tests of the quest took place. This, too, would only be made whole when the Grail Knight came and asked a ritual question which would set in motion a chain of events: the healing of the king, the fructification of the dead land, and something else, less tangible than either of these actions, which would somehow bring transformation to the whole world.

It is this 'something' that has occupied the energies of countless seekers ever since. For within the Grail is seen to reside healing for *all* the ills of creation. With its finding, or with the experience that comes to those who discover its innermost secrets, comes a release

of energy, of selfless love and service, which could change the world for all time – perhaps even bring about the end of time, the rolling-up of the great cosmic chart upon which the history of humanity is written.

ABOVE *Sir Perceval,
the 'perfect fool'
overcomes an
enchantress.*

THE
ELEMENT
LIBRARY
THE
ARTHURIAN
TRADITION

THE HOLY BLOOD

❖

*Sir Galahad receives
sustenance from the Holy
Grail. In the Christian
tradition, the Grail was
used to catch the blood of
Christ's wounds and is
therefore associated with
the Eucharist, when
believers take the blood
and body of Christ
into themselves.*

The single most important element to be
added to the story of the Grail was its
association with the Christian Eucharist. This
shaped and influenced virtually every version
which followed. The Grail was, quite simply,
seen as an outward symbol of Christ's
ministry, of the great sacrifice which brought
God and man into closer proximity than ever
before. It is the unique element of the
Eucharist, the *direct* communion with the
Godhead, which makes the Grail different
from any similar hallowed or sacred object.
From the point of the incarnation, one may
look forward or backward in time without
losing sight of the essential fact: the Grail once
contained Holy Blood of the New Covenant,
caught by Joseph of Arimathaea as he helped
wash the body of Christ after the Cross.

There is no getting away from this, however
one chooses to interpret or reinterpret the
Grail. It can be, and often is, all things to all
men. It is a sublimely mutable image, which
can be turned this way and that while
remaining essentially unchanged.

This does not mean that one has to be a
believer in the Christian dispensation, any
more than it requires that one should become
a pagan. The Grail simply *is*, whatever we
believe or do not believe. And it is this which
makes it an utterly universal symbol, capable
of the widest possible application. It has about
it the stuff of mystery; it is also concerned
with sacrifice, service and the search for the
absolute, whether one calls this God or
Goddess, Divine Spark, or by some even
more abstract term.

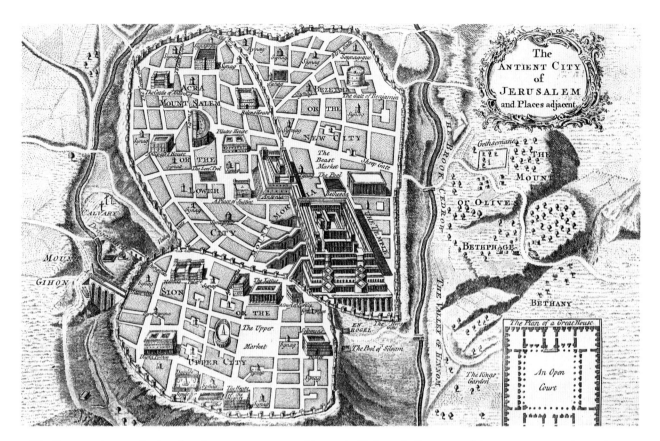

The ANTIENT CITY of JERUSALEM and Places adjacent.

The fact remains, no doubt, that there are similarities between the Celtic, pagan implements and the Christian chalice. These are clearly not accidental. One may assume however, that poets and writers of romances like Chrétien de Troyes and Robert de Borron, as well as all the others who came after them, knew what they were doing. Possibly they were uncertain as to the origins of much of what they wrote. It is equally possible that they knew exactly whence it came. They were, though, first and foremost, creators, not men acting under supernatural guidance or (in many cases) especial piety.

That they were, at the same time, devout, is probable; most men were in the Middle Ages. They must have been aware that the Grail was uncanonical, even though it pertained to the heart of the Christian mystery. The truth is that the image of the Grail continued to change, subtly, throughout the mid-twelfth and mid-thirteenth centuries, when the greatest texts were composed. Chrétien's Grail is enigmatic, unfocused; his continuators, seeing fresh applications, added

something to it. Robert de Borron took it back through time and space to Palestine, adding the dimensions of Joseph of Arimathaea, the Holy Blood, and the bringing of the Cup to Britain. *The Vulgate Cycle*,[71] compiled by Cistercian monks, possibly at the behest of the great theologian Bernard of Clairvaux, further deepened the theology by the introduction of various wandering hermits who interpreted the dreams and visions of the Grail knights, deepening the realisations contained within them. Others, known and unknown, extended the pattern to include all that we now recognise as part of the Grail mythology.

The reason why the twelfth and thirteenth centuries should have been such a formative period in the history of the Grail may in part derive from the fact that this was still an age of comparative doctrinal freedom. Though by no means free to believe whatever they chose, men were less threatened than in succeeding ages. In 1200 there were still some thirty years to go before the Inquisition was established, and a further fifty after that

In an old Spanish text, 'Anales Toledanos', the quest for the Grail took Arthur to Jerusalem and the Holy Land, where he was known as Zitus.

THE
ELEMENT
LIBRARY
THE
ARTHURIAN
TRADITION

before the routine use of torture against suspected heretics was sanctioned by the church.

Once the belief in so-called 'new' ideas was considered heretical, something of the original and striking imagery was lost from the Grail romances written thereafter. Had it not been for the work of an unknown Cistercian, who wrote most, if not all, of the section of *The Vulgate Cycle* in the mid-13th century dealing with the Grail, the myth might well have withered and died. As it was, with the creation of a new character (or at least, his development far beyond any original scope) the whole direction of the Grail legends was changed. Galahad, the Perfect Knight, child of Lancelot and the Grail Princess, had but one destiny: to find the Castle of the Grail and bring about the healing of the Waste Land.

RIGHT *The Chalice Well at Glastonbury, Somerset, the legendary resting place of the Grail.*

❖

THE PURE KNIGHT

RIGHT *Galahad, the pure knight arrives at Arthur's court to claim the Siege Perilous, which has remained empty until his coming.*

❖

The entry of Galahad into the Arthurian tradition is something of a minor miracle; one which Charles Williams, the greatest modern interpreter of the Grail myths, described as one of the most significant literary events of all time. The unknown author of the third part of *The Vulgate Cycle*,[67] Realising the need for a new element to bind the stories into a coherent whole, hit upon the idea of bringing in a Christ-like figure who would literally 'redeem' the legends of their pagan origins. Thus Galahad was born: the sinless, stainless knight best known from Tennyson's nineteenth-century poem as declaring 'my strength is as the strength of ten, because my heart is pure'.

This statement does indeed seem to sum up the character of Galahad, whose name is full of Biblical resonance. It means, literally, 'a heap of testimony' and is understood as referring to the 'accumulated testimony of the Prophets to Christ as Messiah',[43] or the focal point in the heritage of the tradition. Certainly his coming to the court of Arthur is redolent with New Testament detail:

his son, born through an extraordinary substitution, whereby the greatest knight of Arthur's realm engenders the perfect knight on the Princess of the Grail, believing her to be Guinevere.

This in itself is a mystery of great profundity. Guinevere is an aspect of the Great Goddess, the Flower Maiden who rules over the springtime rebirth of the land. She is also the Sorrowful Queen, the Wounded Lady who suffers the burden of evil acts carried out in ignorance of love within the kingdom of Arthur. He, in turn, is the Wounded Lord, the very personification of the land over which he rules – Logres, the mystical realm *within* the geographical boundaries of Britain.

One may see here, links in a causal chain which ultimately bring about the failure of Arthur's dream. Rightly, Galahad should have been the son of Arthur and Guinevere, king and queen, lord and lady. But Arthur begets Mordred upon his half-sister Morgause, and Lancelot is the queen's lover. Thus out of the tangled web of deceit and falsehood comes the redeeming figure of Galahad, allowed by a

❦
In the Meanwhile came in a good old man, and an ancient, clothed all in white, and there was no knight knew from whence he came. And with him he brought a young knight, both on foot, in red arms, without sword or shield, save a scabbard hanging by his side. And these words he said: 'Peace be with you, fair lords'.

(Le Morte D'Arthur, bk XIII, Ch. 3).
❦

All the seats of the Round Table are filled on this occasion, the 454th anniversary of the first Pentecost, with the exception of the Siege Perilous, which had remained empty and veiled since the founding of the Fellowship. Now it is uncovered, and the name Galahad is found to be written upon it in letters of gold. The young knight in red armour takes his place and the mysteries of the Grail begin in earnest: the greatest quest and adventure which the Round Table Knights were ever to attempt. Many would fail, including the great Lancelot. But Galahad is

ABOVE *Galahad's Christian origins are reinforced by his stained glass image at King Arthur's Halls in Tintagel. He is depicted with all the emblematic elements of Christian saints.*

❖

RIGHT *King Bagdemagus wounded by the White Knight after trying to take the holy shield meant for Galahad. The shield was made by Joseph of Arimethaea for King Evelake to fight the saracens. The king and Joseph came to England, where Joseph marked the shield with Christ's blood and dedicated it for Galahad alone.*

❖

THE
ELEMENT
LIBRARY
THE
ARTHURIAN
TRADITION

dispensation of light, to achieve the mystery of the Grail – though not, alas, to bring about the final transformation which would have established Logres as an earthly paradise. Instead, it is given to him to look within the Grail, at which point he expires in an ecstasy of desire which can no longer keep him from union with the absolute. It is left to Perceval, the Perfect Fool, to make possible the continuance of the Grail quest for later ages, and to Bors, the ordinary mortal man and the third of the successful quest knights, to return to the mundane world with word of the great events to which he was witness.

Malory's account, based on the great *Vulgate Quest of the Holy Grail,*[43] is a magnificent parade of images. The knights, departing from Camelot, in the ardour of the quest: their many and extraordinary adventures; the three successful knights who sail on the magical Ship of Solomon, voyaging through time to carry the Grail to Sarras, the Holy City in the east; the failure of Lancelot, of Gawain, and of many others; the sorrowful fate of Perceval's virgin sister, who gives her life-blood for a sick woman, and whose body is carried to the Holy City where she will be interred with Galahad; the return of Perceval to the empty Castle of the Grail, to allow the mystery to begin again – all this and more moves like a dream through the consciousness of those who begin the quest.

For those who go in search of the Grail today do so, whether they know it or not, in the wake of the Arthurian knights, who paved the way and sought the meaning within the great mystery in an open-hearted fashion. They set forth, knowing nothing of the perils that awaited them; and even as word of successive failures reached their ears, they continued the search unabated, establishing new paths, setting out fresh way-markers for those who would follow.

In this, they were far more than characters in a literary cycle of tales. They embodied a series of primary archetypes which have perhaps never been assembled in such a way again; they represent the whole spectrum of human experience, aspiration, failure and ultimate achievement.

Perceval, of the Story of the Grail
~

Perceval is brought up in the forest by his mother, who having lost a husband and three other sons in battle determined that her remaining child shall know nothing of war or contest of arms. Then one day Perceval encounters three of Arthur's knights. Mistaking them at first for angels because of their shining armour, he learns something of the world of men. From this moment nothing will do but that he must leave home in search of adventure. Despairing, his mother clothes him in poor clothes, mounts him on a spavined horse and arms him with a cooking-pot helmet and roughly fashioned spears, in the hope that his foolish appearance will prevent him from encountering any serious harm. She also tells him that if he should encounter any women on the way he should take a ring and a kiss from them, but nothing more.

Perceval's first encounter is with the Damsel of the Tent, who reacts somewhat adversely when he follows his mother's advice. Perceval nevertheless does not forget her. Arriving at Arthur's court he is in time to witness an insult to the queen, when a knight spills wine over her and steals her cup. Determining to take this as his first adventure, Perceval sets out in pursuit. He kills the knight and is in the process of trying to boil the remains in order to obtain his adversary's armour, when he is discovered by an older knight named Governal. This man becomes a father-figure to the young Perceval, and over the next months trains him in the manners and mores of chivalry. Before they part he gives Perceval a second piece of advice: never to speak out of turn or ask foolish questions out of curiosity.

It is this which effects Perceval's next adventure, when he stumbles upon the Castle of the Grail. Within the castle Perceval witnesses a mysterious procession, in which a candelabrum, a spear which drips blood from the point, and a mysterious object called a 'graal', are borne through the hall. In an inner room an ancient man lies, seeming close to death, but who is kept alive by food provided by the 'graal'.

None of this is explained and Perceval, mindful of Governal's advice, forbears to ask its meaning. He goes to bed and next morning wakens to find the castle vanished and himself sleeping on stones. He is then challenged by a hideously ugly maiden who accuses him of failing to take advantage of an opportunity for great good. Outcast and wretched, Perceval wanders for a long while in the wilderness, until he happens to meet a group of pilgrims who remind him that it is Good Friday, when all good Christians should make confession and attend the Eucharist.

Making his way to hermitage in the forest, Perceval learns of the death of his mother, who died of grief when he failed to return or send word of his adventures. Filled with remorse, Perceval prepares to set out once more in search of the mysterious castle of the fisherman.

Anyone who attempts the Grail quest today would do well to study their words and deeds, their successes and failures, as fully as possible. For therein lies much of the teaching of the wise, filtered through a thousand different paths and prejudices, into a great pool of knowledge which lies waiting for those with the courage to plunge into it. Those who do so will perceive many wondrous things – not least of which is a dawning understanding of the mystery behind the Arthurian tradition as a whole, which can only be glimpsed partially and tantalisingly until this point is reached.

Once again it is the sheer *applicability* of the image that gives the Grail such universal relevance. It is not required that those who follow the Grail today adhere to any specific creed or cult – only that they seek the general good, the healing of the barren lands. These things are recognisable and desirable objectives, by whatever terms. Their very enactment causes changes within those who participate in them. By serving, we are served. We grow. The Grail encompasses us with light and an exchange takes place between it and us. In allowing ourselves to be part of its action of healing or redemption, we ourselves partake of its blessing.

This is the great secret of the Grail – which is no secret at all - another paradox in its endlessly paradoxical nature. Everywhere and nowhere simultaneously, it is sought by many, found by only a few. It has been several times withdrawn, yet it still remains. It can heal and it can destroy. It is God and yet not-God. It is a container which is worth far less than what it contains. Of its history, there seems to be no discernible beginning, no assured middle, and certainly no foreseeable end.

The Grail thus represents the most profound puzzle in the whole of the Arthurian tradition. It has only been possible to touch upon some of its mysteries, which are there to be discovered by contemporary seekers, who follow it down the deep ways of the heart, into the realms of wonder and aspiration. There they are met by those who have trodden the way before, whose loving service has led them to stand as foster-parents to those who come after in search of the wisdom of the Grail. This, or itself, has no ending. It is eternal, as the quest itself is eternal. It offers wholeness in the midst of fragmentation. It binds together all who are of its family and its fellowship. It is a gateway between worlds and a bridge to the Divine.

ABOVE *The pinnacle of the knightly quest is the achievement of the Grail.*

LEFT *Galahad has a vision of the Grail guarded by creatures with both Otherworldly and Christian overtones.*

7

AVALON
AND THE
FAERY REALMS

Paths to the Land Beyond

Bardsey Island, off the coast of Angelsey, believed by some to be the site of Merlin's secret observatory.

❖

And I will fare to Avalun, to the fairest of all maidens, to Argante the queen, an elf most fair, and she shall make my wounds all sound; make me all whole with healing draughts. And afterwards I will come again to my kingdom, and dwell with Britons with mickle joy.

Layamon, Brut

THE DREAM OF THE OTHERWORLD

It is virtually impossible to explore any of the traditions relating to Arthur and the Grail without encountering some aspect of the Otherworld. The knights in their wanderings continually stray out of the realms of men into the faery world, or else encounter the denizens of the Hollow Hills who have emerged with the intention of testing all whom they meet. Why the members of the Otherworld should seek to do this has never been successfully answered. In part it seems to be out of nothing more than a sense of pure mischief; but at a deeper level it appears that the people of the Otherworld, in their shy way, actively *seek* the companionship of humans – though they are less willing to share the secrets of the inner realms or to give Otherworldly power to mortals.

In one of the many stories featuring Gawain, who has a relationship with the Otherworld perhaps unique among the knights, he meets a dangerous figure called the Carl of Carlisle. Gawain accompanies him on a journey which takes them at once inside the Hollow Hills, where they seem to travel through a world as real as the one they have left, save that the adventures which follow are touched with a degree of strangeness unusual even for the Champion of the Goddess.[59]

In another text, *Sone of Nausay*,[44] the hero, who is pictured as a genuine historical personage possibly from the region of Alsace, journeys with the King of Norway through a land filled with strange creatures to an island where they find the body of Joseph of Arimathaea, perfectly preserved, together with the Grail itself! The setting is wholly Otherworldly however, and the island, which is named *Galoche* (probably a corruption of the French word for 'Welsh') is one among many such Otherworldly places found throughout the Arthurian and Celtic traditions.

Merlin, also, had his island retreat, which is sometimes located at Bardsey, off the coast of Angelsey. Here he was believed to have his observatory and to guard the Thirteen Treasures of Britain, which included an inexhaustible cauldron, a collection of magical weaponry, and a great horn which had once belonged to the god Bran – who also, incidentally, had an enchanted island where time stood still and where food and drink were provided from an unseen source.

Each of these places represented a deep-seated urge for Otherness, for a place where the laws of the natural world no longer obtained; where anything was possible, and even the poor might become rich, or the dispossessed get back their lost standing in the eyes of the world. Later, this dream was to be replaced by another – that of Heaven, the paradise where the good were assured of an eternity of rest and peace. However, the Celtic Otherworld was altogether a more robust place where the simple pleasures – ample food and drink, beautiful women, heroic men, great combats in which neither opponent received fatal wounds – abounded. One place summed up this Otherworldliness more than any other: Avalon.

Arthur sleeps in the Hall of Avalon guarded by the queens of the Otherworld as forces from the mundane world try to break in on all sides.

THE
ELEMENT
LIBRARY
THE
ARTHURIAN
TRADITION

THE ISLAND OF APPLES

Among all the hundreds of names attached to the Celtic Otherworld, that of Avalon must be the most evocative. It is the place to which tradition ascribes the last resting place of Arthur. There he waits still for the day when he is called back to serve the needs of the land, to begin again the work that was left unfinished after the ending of the Grail quest and the bloody slaughter of the Round Table Fellowship at Camlan.

Many have sought to discover the whereabouts of this fabled place, and tradition has, since the Middle Ages, associated it with the Somerset town of Glastonbury, which has been called 'this holiest earth'. Here Joseph of Arimathaea is believed to have come, bearing the precious Grail, and to have established the first Christian community there within living memory of Christ. And here saints such as Patrick, Bridget and Columba are said to have lived for a time.

It may be unwise to seek a physical place for something as elemental as Avalon. But in the time of the Celtic war-lords when Somerset

❖

Glastonbury Tor broods over Glastonbury, long considered to be the real site of the mythical Avalon or very closely associated with it.

was known as 'The Summer Country' and was more than half in the Otherworld, Glastonbury (a Saxon name) was known as *Yniswitrin*, a Welsh name which has been interpreted as meaning 'The Island of Glass', ruled over by Avalach, who is also called *Rex Avalonis*, King of Avalon. He is the father of Morgan, described in another text as 'The Royal Virgin of Avalon' – though that title can only be that of a hereditary guardian rather than a literal description.

So *Yniswitrin* became Avalon, the Island of Apples, a place of wonder and mystery, where it was known that some great and mysterious object was kept, guarded, perhaps by a college of priestesses under the leadership of Morgan – she who was elsewhere known as Arthur's sister and a servant of the Goddess.

Thus an inner landscape was outlined within the Arthurian tradition. Logres, the mystical heart of Britain, with its royal castles at Camelot, Caerleon and Carlisle, its great forests in which the Fellowship of the Round Table wandered in search of adventure and its

magical springs and wells guarded by Otherworldly maidens of surpassing beauty. And at the centre, somehow, lay Avalon, the magical isle which was a doorway onto the lands of faery, to the people of the Sidhe, who sent forth their representatives into the lands of men, to try and test them – and sometimes to lead them back into the deep places of the earth, where the Old Gods still dwelled as they had done since the beginning of time.

The Arthurian kingdom was always on the edge of faery. When Arthur set out in his ship *Pridwen* with his band of wondrously endowed warriors, they sailed to an island where the Cauldron of Rebirth was kept, guarded by nine muses, and by the warriors of the Otherworld. Nor a far cry from this to another island, ruled by Morgan and her sisters, where a vessel was housed that could give life and healing to those in sore need.

But Avalon was more even than this. It was a place where eternity touched the earth, where anything could happen – and did. It was both a gateway between the worlds and the home of the deepest mysteries of Britain. It was one of 'The Fortunate Isles', a place of apple trees and the perfume of flowers. Malory calls it 'the vale of Avilion', and Geoffrey of Monmouth describes it in detail.

The island of apples … gets its name from the fact that it produces all things of itself; the fields there have no need of the ploughs of the farmers and all cultivation is lacking except what nature provides. Of its own accord it produces grain and grapes, and apple trees grow in the woods from the close-clipped grass. The ground of its own accord produces everything instead of merely grass, and people live there a hundred years or more. There nine sisters rule by a pleasing set of laws those who come to them from our country … Thither after the battle of Camlan we took the wounded Arthur … Morgan received us with fitting honour, and in her chamber she placed the king on a golden bed and with her own hand she uncovered his honourable wound and … at length she said that health could be restored to him if he stayed with her for a long time and made use of her healing art.

This Avalon is a place of healing, a realm of peace where even the enmity of Morgan for Arthur no longer holds good. Here too belongs Nimue, the damsel of the lake who enchanted Merlin and finally imprisoned him in a cavern beneath a great rock. The Queens of Norgales and of the Waste Land are said to come here, connecting the Otherworld with the Kingdom of the Grail.

Another text, the *Gesta Regum Britanniae*,[64] which actually postdates Geoffrey by a few decades, describes Avalon in terms which link it even more explicitly to the realms of faery.

This wondrous island is girdled by the ocean; it lacks no good things; no thief, reiver or enemy lurks in ambush there. No snow falls; neither Summer nor Winter rages uncontrollably, but unbroken peace and harmony and the gentle warmth of unbroken Spring. Not a flower is lacking, neither lilies, rose nor violet; the apple-tree bears flowers and fruit together on one bough. Youth and maiden live together in that place without blot or shame. Old age is unknown; there is neither sickness nor suffering – everything is full of joy. No one selfishly keeps anything to himself; here everything is shared.[52]

In other cultures this would have been called an earthly paradise; to the Celts it was the Otherworld, a place as simple and real as one might find in the realms of men. We may wonder at a realm where sickness and sorrow, old age and misery are banished; where men and women live together in peace and harmony, and where all things are provided from the goodness and plenty of the earth. To the people who helped create the Arthurian tradition as we know it, such places lay merely over the next hill.

Such a paradise seems a wholly fitting resting place for Arthur, who sought to create just such a perfect realm in the world, only to be defeated by human weaknesses and failings which the Otherworld were not subject.

The faeryland depicted in folk story is a pale echo of the beauty of the otherworld of Avalon.

❖

THE
ELEMENT
LIBRARY
THE
ARTHURIAN
TRADITION

THE WONDROUS REALM

The Sick-bed of Cuchulainn
~

I WENT IN THE TWINKLING OF AN EYE
INTO A MARVELLOUS COUNTRY WHERE I HAD BEEN
BEFORE.
I REACHED A CAIRN OF TWENTY ARMIES,
AND THERE I FOUND LABRAID OF THE LONG HAIR.

I FOUND HIM SITTING ON THE CAIRN,
A GREAT MULTITUDE OF ARMS ABOUT HIM.
ON HIS HEAD HIS BEAUTIFUL FAIR HAIR
WAS DECKED WITH AN APPLE OF GOLD.
ALTHOUGH THE TIME WAS LONG SINCE MY LAST VISIT
HE RECOGNISED ME BY MY FIVE-FOLD PURPLE MANTLE.
SAID HE, 'WILT THOU COME WITH ME
INTO THE HOUSE WHERE DWELLS FAILBE THE FAIR?'

AT THE DOOR TOWARD THE WEST
ON THE SIDE TOWARD THE SETTING SUN,
THERE IS A TROOP OF GREY HORSES WITH DAPPLED
MANES,
AND ANOTHER TROOP OF HORSES, PURPLE-BROWN.
AT THE DOOR TOWARD THE EAST
ARE THREE TREES OF PURPLE GLASS.
FROM THEIR TOPS A FLOCK OF BIRDS SING A SWEET
DRAWN-OUT SONG
FOR THE CHILDREN WHO LIVE IN THE ROYAL
STRONGHOLD.
AT THE ENTRANCE TO THE ENCLOSURE IS A TREE
FROM WHOSE BRANCHES COMES BEAUTIFUL AND
HARMONIOUS MUSIC.
IT IS A TREE OF SILVER, WHICH THE SUN ILLUMINES;
IT GLISTENS LIKE GOLD.

THERE IS A CAULDRON OF INVIGORATING MEAD,
FOR THE USE OF THE INMATES OF THE HOUSE.
IT NEVER GROWS LESS; IT IS A CUSTOM
THAT IT SHOULD BE FULL FOREVER.
THERE IS A WOMAN IN THE NOBLE PALACE.
THERE IS NO WOMAN LIKE HER IN ERIN [IRELAND].
WHEN SHE GOES FORTH YOU SEE HER FAIR HAIR.
SHE IS BEAUTIFUL AND ENDOWED WITH MANY GIFTS.

Anon, 9th-century Irish poem

Avalon then is like the perfect, balanced state of being, reached sometimes in meditation, or with the practice of certain religious disciplines. It is a place sought by those in quest of the Grail and of the Cave of the Heart; or as Dion Fortune put it: 'Sir Lancelot seeking one thing and Sir Galahad another, still they come to Avalon'.[15] It is the heart from which all the Arthurian mysteries are generated – and to which all who seek to

understand those mysteries must come. Here, at the Round Table of the Stars, a gathering of mighty cosmic beings is established, part of a tradition which is nowhere written about but which was part of the inner history of the land long before Arthur, either as war-lord or king, was ever heard of. Known also as 'The Dweller in Avalon', these archetypal figures send out a call which is answered in time by all who are drawn to study the Arthurian tradition.

The power of the inner realms is thus conveyed, in a broad ray, outward from the centre, until it percolates towards a cosmic goal hinted at in the mysteries of the Grail and in the deeds of the Round Table Fellowship. A word, whispered in Avalon, becomes a trumpet call in the ears of those who seek the good of the world and the furtherance of mankind.

But this can only happen if we will it, if the desire for good, for the healing of the wounded land and the wounded hearts of mankind, is strong enough to penetrate the darkness which obscures so much of the world at this time. Belief in, and practice of, the spiritual disciplines taught in the myths of the Grail, in the Cave of the Heart, and in the deeds of the Round Table Fellowship in the Lands Adventurous, can cause great and lasting changes in the world – perhaps beginning, in however small a way, with the enormous tasks of restoring the Waste Lands, of healing the Wounded King, or of re-establishing the Logres within Britain in the hearts and minds of its people.

The myths of Arthur and the Round Table Fellowship embody this dream in tales of valour and chivalry, of quest and achievement. As the great Celticist Jean Markale put it:

… many of the epic tales of war in the British and Irish traditions refer to symbolic conflicts. The symbols take various forms. We find brother fighting brother, hero against hero, gods against men and gods against fairy people. There are expeditions to the Other World, which may lie just around the corner or far over the water; and quests for mysterious objects which must be found for the hero to keep his strength or his honour. But all of them represent a concerted attempt to reconcile the contradictions inherent in social life and man's subsequent sense of alienation in its most profound diversity … Celtic epic portrays the great inner struggles of man and his conflicts with his environment through real battles against hostile forces.[49]

It was the struggle which gave rise to the Arthurian tradition. Through a study of its archetypal stories, we may begin to see ways in which the problems of our own time can be solved.

LEFT *All mythic realms connect, and here Arthurian legend and Greek myth meet. Arthur is shown with Aegle, one of the Hesperides, nymphs of the evening who lived in the far west and guarded a magic orchard of golden apples.*

❖

OPPOSITE FAR LEFT *A ninth-century Irish poem describes the otherworld in terms that are reflected in the later Arthurian texts.*

❖

8

THE
UNENDING
SONG

Arthur in the Modern World

*T*hus Arthur had himself borne to Avalon and he told his people that they should await him
and he would return. And the Britons came back to Carduel and waited home more than
forty years before they would take a king, for they believed always that he would return.
But this you know in truth that some have since seen him hunting in the forest, and they have
heard his dogs with him and some have hoped for a long time that he would return.

Didot Perceval

A MUTABLE IMAGE

From the start, the Arthurian tradition has been subject to constant, though often subtle, change. The heroic mould which gave us the earliest figure of Arthur, gave way to that of the chivalric king ruling over an elegant medieval court. Later ages presented a more political framework, with spurious prophecies, attributed to Merlin, declaring for the latest regime.

The Tudors in particular leant heavily on the existence of Arthur in their family tree to bolster their claims to the throne of Britain. Henry VII was extolled as 'The beast from North Wales, a man of renown … of the blood of Arthur … [Winner of] the great joy predicted by Merlin'. While Thomas Churchyard, in his book *The Worthiness of Wales* in 1587, referred to Elizabeth I as:

She that sits in regall Throne,
With Sceptre, Sword, and Crowne.
(Who came from Arthur's rase and lyne).

Still later, in 1610, the playwright Ben Jonson wrote a pageant called *The Speeches at Prince Henry's Barriers*, in which he described James I as the monarch who 'Wise, temperate, just, and stout, claims Arthur's

ABOVE *James I of England and VI of Scotland, regarded himself as a lineal descendant of Arthur.*

❖

BELOW *The Attainment (1895-6), designed by Edward Burne-Jones and woven by William Morris. Arthurian subjects fascinated the Pre-Raphaelite artists, whose work triggered an enormous revival of interest in the legends.*

seat', a reference no doubt to the then popular epigram which declared that:

Charles James Steuart
Claimes Arthurs Seate

On the literary horizon Arthur's star waned for a time. Spenser devoted the first part of his epic *The Faerie Queene* to the deeds of young Prince Arthur, and clearly drew upon Malory and earlier sources for his inspiration. Merlin made a brief appearance in the story of *Don Quixote*, by Miguel Cervantes. Milton contemplated an Arthurian epic but changed his mind in favour of the story of Adam and Eve. Later, the visionary poet and painter William Blake referred to Arthur and Merlin in some of his most important works.

In the nineteenth century came the birth of Romanticism, and with this the figures of Arthur, Guinevere, Lancelot and Tristan underwent a renaissance. The Poet Laureate, Alfred Tennyson, wrote a long series of 'idylls', poems whose sonorous rhythms brought back something of the original power of the romances – for all that, Tennyson endowed all the knights with solid Victorian values and all but dressed Arthur in a frock coat and stove-pipe hat!

THE
ELEMENT
LIBRARY
THE
ARTHURIAN
TRADITION

ABOVE *Gloriana, or Elizabeth I, the eponymous Faerie Queene, heroine and dedicatee of Spenser's Arthurian allegory of Elizabethan life.*

ABOVE RIGHT *Don Quixote, the myopic myth-enshrouded hero of Cervantes' novel (1605) lived his life by the chivalrous ideals of the Arthurian knights.*

Throughout the rest of the era, Arthurian themes dominated the arts of poetry, music and painting. The Pre-Raphaelite Brotherhood, whose numbers included Edward Burne-Jones and William Morris, produced many striking pictures based on Arthurian themes on the subject. Poetry good, bad and indifferent, poured forth and was avidly read. The magic and beauty of the stories wove a spell over the drab Victorian age, touching again and again the deepest levels of human experience.

A NEW BEGINNING

With the dawning of the twentieth century came war and destruction on a scale scarcely dreamed of before. A new breed of artist began to emerge, and among them were many who turned again to the images and stories of the Arthurian tradition for inspiration.

The poet and painter David Jones was one of this new breed. He painted a number of

extraordinary pictures on Arthurian themes – picturing the Grail Mass taking place in a bombed-out chapel in the middle of the new Waste Land of the Western Front. In his great poem, *In Parenthesis*,[28] he portrayed First World War soldiers fighting side by side with Arthurian heroes. And in the work which followed it, *The Anathemata*,[27] he produced an

extraordinary evocation of Britain from its
geological past to a semi-mythic eternity,
bringing in the themes of Arthur and the Grail
with tremendous force and vitality.

Modern techniques of archaeology, and
further research into the sparse documents of
the sixth and seventh centuries, began to
reveal more of the reality behind the earliest
heroic tales. The so-called Dark Ages were no
longer so opaque, and with this ever-widening
pool of knowledge to draw upon, once again
novelists and poets drew on the Arthurian
tradition for their inspiration.

A number of memorable historical novels
appeared from the 1940s onwards. Edward
Frankland wrote a detailed and poetic account
of the historical Arthur in his Book *The Bear of
Britain*,[16] and this was followed by such works
as *The Great Captains* by Henry Treece,[85]
which told the story from the viewpoint of
Mordred: *Porius* by John Cowper Powys[66] – a
vast sprawling romance worthy of the best of
its medieval forbears but wholly
contemporary; and perhaps best of all *The
Sword at Sunset* by Rosemary Sutcliff,[80] which
evoked a totally human Arthur, touched with
the magic of a forgotten age, tragic and noble,
still striving towards the ideal kingdom of
Malory's *Le Morte D'Arthur* and the writers of
The Vulgate Cycle.

T. H. White published a quartet of books
under the overall title *The Once and Future*

King,[90] taking the Latin epitaph said to be
carved upon the tomb where Arthur's bones
had never lain. In this book, White sets out to
retell the story as Malory had given it, but
with certain significant changes. The first
book, *The Sword in the Stone*, tells the story of
Arthur's childhood and training at the hands
of Merlin – or rather, as White spells it,
Merlyn. This rather comical old gentleman,
who lives backwards and is thus enabled to see
the future which, to him, has already
happened, seems a far cry from the Merlin of
earlier times. Yet his magic is no less potent.
Arthur learns the things which he needs to fit
him for the great task ahead by taking the
shapes of bird, beast and insect, each of which
shows him the foolishness of the ways of men.

ABOVE *Another
claimant for Arthur's
bones is a memorial slab
beside the River Camel
at Slaughter Bridge
in Cornwall. This
is the possible site
of the battle of Camlan,
where Arthur was
fatally wounded.*

❖

LEFT *Trystan, by
David Jones, shows
Tristan and the future
queen Isolt on their
momentous voyage from
Ireland to Cornwall.*

❖

THE
ELEMENT
LIBRARY
THE
ARTHURIAN
TRADITION

But this light-hearted beginning becomes gradually darkened in the books which follow. *The Queen of Air and Darkness* concentrates on the figure of Morgause, and the childhood of her sons Gawain, Gareth, Gaheries and Agravaine. The book culminates in the birth of Mordred, whose coming is to spell destruction for the Arthurian world. The third book, *The Ill-Made Knight*, tells the story of Lancelot and Guinevere with a degree of passion and psychological realism seldom attained before or since. Finally, *The Candle in the Wind* tells the story of the downfall of the Round Table, the war against Lancelot and the doom-laden end to the tale. A fifth volume, left unfinished by White at his death, was published later as *The Story of Merlyn*.[91] It tells what happens when the old wizard returns to Arthur's tent on the eve of the battle of Camlan. He takes his protegé through a further series of transformations which equip him for a new beginning *after* his time in Avalon. It is marred by White's bitter response to the imminent war with Germany, but it nevertheless contains some of his finest writing, taking Arthur beyond the darkness in which his dream ends, towards a new source of light.

Poets also did not neglect the tradition. Another Poet Laureate, John Masefield, produced a series of powerful lyrics in *Midsummer Night*,[51] mingling the heroic and the romantic elements of the old stories in a wholly new way. Charles Williams, one of the august group known as the Inklings, who included J.R.R. Tolkien and C.S. Lewis among their number, wrote what is still the most powerful and magical series of poems on the theme of the Grail, creating an entire world, stretching from the negative realm of P'o L'u, the realm of negative evil, to the great city of the Grail at Sarras. No simple account can give any real idea of the magisterial quality of these poems, which appeared in two volumes, *Taliesin through Logres* and *The Region of the Summer Stars*[92]. The poem shown on the right gives only a taste, which should be supplemented by a reading of all the works, together with the forthcoming book by Gareth Knight[33].

In the extract from one of Williams' poems, Merlin and his twin sister Brisen, who stand for Time and Space in Williams' universe and are the daughters of Nimure (Nature), enact a magical operation to assist in the founding of the Arthurian kingdom.

Another distinguished poet, John Heath Stubbs, gave his vision of Arthur in a wide-ranging epic entitled *Artorious*,[24] combining myth, romance, and the heroic in a subtle blend. More recently still there has been a positive spate of novels: *Mists of Avalon* by Marion Zimmer Bradley;[4] *Down the Long Wind* by Gillian Bradshaw, a trilogy of novels on Merlin by Mary Stewart,[72, 73, 74] and another by Stephen Lawhead, *Taliesin, Merlin*, and

❖

A woodcut, 'He Frees the Waters' by David Jones, depicts the healing of the Wasteland by Christ in the form of a unicorn.

The Calling of Taliesin
~

THE CONE'S SHADOW OF EARTH FELL INTO SPACE,
AND INTO (OTHER THAN SPACE) THE THIRD HEAVEN.
IN THE THIRD HEAVEN ARE THE LIVING UNRIVEN TRUTHS,
CLIMAX TRANQUIL IN VENUS. MERLIN AND BRISEN
HEARD, AS IN FAINT BEE-LIKE HUMMING
ROUND THE CONE'S POINT,
THE FEELING INTELLECT HASTEN
TO FASTEN ON THE EARTH'S IMAGE; IN THE THIRD HEAVEN
THE STONES OF THE WASTE GLIMMERED
LIKE SUMMER STARS.
BETWEEN WOOD AND WASTE THE YOKED
CHILDREN OF NIMUE
OPENED THE RITE; THEY INVOKED THE THIRD HEAVEN.
HEARD IN THE FAR HUMMING OF THE SPIRITUAL
INTELLECT,
TO THE BUILDING OF LOGRES AND THE COMING OF THE
LAND OF THE TRINITY
WHICH IS CALLED SARRAS IN MAPS OF THE SOUL, MERLIN
MADE PREPARATION...
HE LIFTED THE FIVE TIMES CROSS-INCISED ROD AND BEGAN
INCANTATION; IN THE TONGUE OF BROCELIANDE
ADJURING ALL THE PRIMAL ATOMS OF EARTH
TO SHAPE THE BORDERS OF LOGRES, TO THE
DISPENSATION
OF CARBONEK TO CAERLEON, OF CAERLEON TO CAMELOT,
TO THE UNION
OF KING PELLES AND KING ARTHUR...

Charles Williams, *Taliesin Through Logres*

Arthur.[38, 39, 40] All these works have introduced a powerful strain of magic into the retelling of the stories, thus widening and deepening their application to the contemporary seeker. Marion Zimmer Bradley tells her story from the viewpoint of Morgan le Fay, evoking a rich vision of Avalon as a Faery world which is gradually floating further away from the historical realm of Arthur. The same author also invokes the shadow of Atlantis in the early part of the book, taking up an idea first put forward in a received text by Dion Fortune, that Arthur's mother Igrain was one of the few who escaped (along with Merlin) from the drowned continent – bringing with her the blood-line and magical knowledge of the most ancient and advanced civilisation that has ever flourished on earth.

Stephen Lawhead expands on this concept still further in his trilogy by making the survivors of the cataclysm found various communities at Glastonbury and elsewhere in Britain – foundations which become synonymous in the minds of the original inhabitants with the *Sidhe*.

Gillian Bradshaw, in her series of books about Gawain, again introduces magical themes into the narrative, giving to her hero the task of finding and wielding the magical sword of light under the aegis of the god Lugh. In doing so, she harks back to a tradition which makes Gawain the wielder of Excalibur, gifted to him by Arthur for a time in the wars against the Saxons.

Merlin, in Mary Stewart's trilogy, is more of a modern magician than the inspired druid of earlier texts. Yet he is a recognisable descendant of the Merlin Ambrosius written about by Geoffrey of Monmouth. He falls into inspired trances and suffers the terrible agonies of the gifted psychic who sees all, but is helpless to do more than watch as the kingdom he helped to create falls back into the darkness from which it emerged.

Contemporary cinema likewise has not neglected the realms of Arthur. At least one recent work, *Excalibur*, directed by John Boorman, and co-written with Rospo Pallenburg, gives a marvellously rich account of the whole cycle from Arthur's birth to the Last Battle. Though compressed at times to a point where it is difficult to comprehend, the sub-text of the film has a unity rare in any Arthurian work. It makes significant use of the symbolism of the Grail quest and successfully demonstrates the links between Arthur and the Wounded King, who in this version are one. It also contains the best portrayal of Merlin to date, as a wise, quirky, sorrowful figure who is the last Dragon Priest of Britain and draws upon the immense power of the inner earth to bring about his magical operations.

Arthurian romance retains a strong grip on the 20th-century imagination. This is a scene from John Boorman's film Excalibur (1981).
❖

A MAGICAL DIMENSION

A common factor in many of the modern works discussed here is their magical and esoteric significance. Thus Diana Paxson in her novel of Tristan, *The White Raven*,[65] draws upon her own knowledge of magic as a priestess of the Covenant of the Goddess. Likewise, the magical descriptions contained in Charles Williams' writings draw upon his own years in the Magical Order of the Golden Dawn.

THE
ELEMENT
LIBRARY
THE
ARTHURIAN
TRADITION

As long ago as the 1890s this prestigious group, which included A.E. Waite, W.B. Yeats and (briefly) Aleister Crowley among its numbers, were drawing upon the Arthurian tradition in their magical operations. This was continued by Dion Fortune in the Society of the Inner Light,[15] and thereafter by the Servants of the Light School of Qabalistic Science, and by individuals such as Gareth Knight, R.J. Stewart and the present writer.

It is part of the ultimate value and importance of the Arthurian tradition that, because it is founded upon esoteric principles embodying such varied archetypal forces, it is unusually apposite for magical work. An example of this, to which the present author was witness, took place during a weekend workshop in Gloucestershire in 1982. At this workshop, a tremendous pool of energy was built up, using the group consciousness of the fifty to sixty people present. When this had been allowed to create its own vortex of power, the operator leading the group proceeded to 'summon' Arthur, Guinevere, Merlin and Morgan back from the inner realms. The immediacy and power of the response was total. The Arthurian archetypes were quite literally present among the group, and remained so for some time after. In a certain sense, the Sleeping Lord was recalled from Avalon and sent forth again into the world to work for the restoration of the kingdom. The same group continued and strengthened this work at actual sites with

Arthurian associations, at further group meetings and by individuals working alone.

Another first-hand account adds further details:

❧

The prophecy of the return of Arthur was fulfilled that night at the Camelot we had built. After reading of Tennyson's Morte d'Arthur, we invited back into our company the redeemed archetypes of the Round Table. We sat silently, for what seemed an age, invoking the personages with whom we had become so familiar throughout the weekend, sending them forth to intercede with the troubled world of our own times. It was truly an awesome and splendid thing that we did. The power which we invoked was both visible and perceptible in every sense: the candles on the altar shimmering with a radiance greater than their own. None of us wanted to leave: we were gripped, not by fear, but by a longing to remain. Then one by one the company dispersed to bear into the world the substance of what we had experienced, to continue the work of the Round Table within our own sphere of life.[5]

❧

This operation culminated in a large-scale working in 1987, intended to bring about the Restoration of the Courts of Joy. This is a deeply magical place in which the four Hallows of the Grail myth, Cup, Spear, Stone and Sword, were set once more at power-points in the body of Logres – there to work actively for the healing of the land and those who dwell upon it.[56]

There are many other valid systems with which to work, and the present author does not wish to denigrate any of these by concentrating on the Arthurian tradition, which, though it is grounded in our native soil, has become universal through its wider application. No matter in what part of the world those who wish to explore it may live, the same values still obtain. The heart legends of many lands have their own Arthurs, their own Merlins, their own rich heritage of traditions which draw upon the same basic source.

In this country, the enduring flame and magical potency of Arthur continues to burn with a steady flame. The traditions which speak of Arthur as the Sleeping Lord, the tutelary spirit of inner Britain, embody a reality of great power.

❧

How long has he been the
sleeping lord?
are the clammy ferns
his rustling vallance
does the buried rowan
ward him from evil, or
does he ward the tanglewood
and the denizens of the wood
are the stunted oaks his gnarled guard
or are their knarred limbs
strong with his sap?...
Does the land wait the sleeping lord
or is the wasted land
that very lord who sleeps?

❧

David Jones, *The Sleeping Lord*

THE
ELEMENT
LIBRARY
THE
ARTHURIAN
TRADITION

GLOSSARY OF

ARTHURIAN CHARACTERS

AGRAVAIN Son of Lot and Morgause, the third of the Orkney brothers, who included Gawain, Gaheries and Gareth. Less reliable than the others, Agravain was involved in the plot against Lancelot which brought down the chivalry of the Round Table. He met his death at the hands of Lancelot in the fighting outside the queen's chamber.

AMBROSIUS AURELIANUS Vortigern's successor and brother of Uther.

ARTHUR Son of Uther and Igrain. It was said that his mother had been among those who escaped from Atlantis before the great continent sank. Others maintained that she had faery blood. Certainly Uther possessed the ancient blood of the British kings, being descended from a line of rulers. Arthur became the sacred king of Britain on drawing a sword from a stone – not Excalibur as is sometimes believed, but a symbol of his right to rule arranged by Merlin. Merlin brought about Arthur's birth by disguising Uther to look like Igrain's husband Gorlois.

KING ARTHUR

BEDEVERE Knight of the Round Table. One of the first to join the Fellowship. He became the Butler to the court, organising feasts and tournaments along with the irascible Kay. A warrior in his own right, he was with Arthur to the end and finally threw the enchanted sword Excalibur back into the lake from which it had come.

BERTILAK Knight transformed by Morgan into the likeness of the Green Knight. He stands for the principle of winter. In his alternate guise he is a vegetation god whose task it is to test and then initiate Gawain into the mysteries of the Goddess. Lady Bercilak,

his wife, was forced to attempt the seduction of Gawain so that he would betray the vows of chivalry and thus damage the reputation of the Round Table. At a deeper level, she represents one of the aspects of the Goddess whose role as temptress was also designed to initiate Gawain into her service.

BLAISE The master of Merlin. In the Didot Perceval,[70] Merlin reports to Blaise before retiring. A shadowy figure, described as a monk or hermit in most texts, but in reality suggesting a more ancient and primal figure who taught Merlin the secret arts.

BORS Cousin of Lancelot. One of the strongest knights of the Round Table, he became the third of the trio of successful Grail Knights. Steadiness and dependability were his chief aspects. He alone returned to Camelot at the end of the great quest to tell Arthur what had occurred. Later, he refused to defend Guinevere against accusations of adultery, changed his mind and then was relieved by Lancelot, who appeared at the last moment to save her. Surviving most of the Fellowship, he died in Palestine fighting in the Crusades.

BRAN Ancestral King of Britain. One of the powerful titanic gods who ruled the land before the coming of Arthur. He also prefigures the Wounded King of the later Stories. At his death he commanded that his head be cut off and carried to the island of Gwales where it continued to oraculate for many years, until one of the company who accompanied it opened a forbidden door, at which point the head fell silent and began to decay. It was then carried to the White Mount in London and buried there in accordance with Bran's wishes, so that he might continue to defend the country against invasion. Arthur later ordered the head dug up so that he alone was considered the defender of Britain.

BRANGAINE The companion of Isolt of Cornwall who gives Tristan and her mistress the love potion brewed by Isolt's mother intended for the wedding night of Isolt with Mark. After Tristan becomes the lover of her mistress Branwyn agrees to substitute herself on the wedding night so that Mark will never know that his wife was no longer a virgin.

Brisen: the nurse of Elaine of Corbenic. Brisen arranges the deception by which Galahad is engendered, giving Lancelot a drugged drink which causes him to believe that he is with Guinevere. Elaine brings up Galahad then sends him to the care of nuns at Amesbury.

CULHWCH Early Celtic hero whose quest for Olwen White-Footprint, daughter of Yspadden Chief-Giant, lead him to request aid from his cousin Arthur. A fantastic collection of heroes with Otherworldly abilities are dispatched to help the youth, and a mass of fragmentary hero tales are drawn upon for the adventures that follow.

DAGONET Arthur's court jester who became a Knight of the Round Table and whose gentle mockery made him among the most popular figures in the Arthurian panoply. He became an especial friend of Tristan, more than once rescuing him from capture by Mark.

DINDAINE The sister of Perceval, who accompanies the Grail Knights and eventually sacrifices herself in order to heal a leprous woman. Her body is carried in their magical Ship of Solomon to the sacred city of Sarras, where it is buried alongside that of Galahad. As the only woman involved in the Grail quest, her role is of the utmost importance. She represents, along with Elaine of Corbenic, the feminine mysteries of the Grail.

ECTOR The foster-father of Arthur. He brought up the young king in ignorance of his identity after being entrusted with the child by Merlin.

ELAINE OF ASTOLAT The maiden by whose father Lancelot is secretly armed for a tournament. She falls in love with the famous knight and when she realises that he will never return that love, she starves herself to death. Her body is put into a boat and carried down river to Camelot where all are saddened by her fate.

ELAINE OF CORBENIC The daughter of Pelles, of the Grail Family. Brisen gives Lancelot a drugged potion so that he sleeps with Elaine, believing her to be Guinevere. When he discovers the deception he goes out of his mind for a time, but is finally discovered and healed by Elaine. The result of their union is a child, Galahad. Elaine features as the Grail Princess under a number of other names in the rest of the Arthurian sagas.

GAHERIES Son of Lot and Morgause. The second of the Orkney brothers, he discovers that Morgause has taken the knight Lamorack as her love, and discovering them in bed together cuts off his mother's head in a fit of passion. He later dies at Lancelot's hand in the battle to rescue Guinevere from the stake.

GALAHAD Son of Elaine of Corbenic and Lancelot. He surpasses his father in both chivalry and purity of life, becoming the achiever of the Grail along with Perceval and Bors. His relationship with his father is touching and enlightening, and his last words are to tell Bors to 'remember me to my father Sir Lancelot'.

SIR GALAHAD

GALAHAUT THE HAUT PRINCE Lord of the Kingdom of Surluse. He wars against Arthur in the early days of the young king's reign, but finally surrenders after observing the chivalry of Lancelot, whose devoted follower he then becomes. Finally, believing Lancelot dead, he refuses to eat and starves himself to death. He is buried with honour at Lancelot's castle of Joyous Gard.

GARETH OF ORKNEY Third son of Lot and Morgause, he comes anonymously to court and is called Beaumains (Fair Hands) by Kay, who puts him to work in the kitchens. He requests that he be allowed to go on the

THE
ELEMENT
LIBRARY
THE
ARTHURIAN
TRADITION

adventure of Linet and distinguishes himself greatly, fighting a series of multi-coloured knights. He is knighted by Lancelot whose devoted follower he becomes, and is tragically slain by the great knight during the battle to rescue Guinevere from the stake.

GAWAIN Son of King Lot of Orkney. The eldest of the Orkney brothers, he was the greatest knight at the Arthurian court until the coming of Lancelot. His reputation suffered due to his allegiance to the Goddess, whose champion and lover he became after the initiation tests of the Green Knight, and his marriage to Ragnall. The death of his brothers at Lancelot's hands drove him to become the bitterest foe of his once greatest friend. He died from wounds received in a fight that Lancelot never wished for. His ghost appeared to Arthur before the battle of Camlan.

GORLOIS Duke of Cornwall, first husband of Igrain. He fights a bitter war with Uther and is finally slain in a foray from the castle of Tintagel. Merlin then disguises Uther so that he has the appearance of Gorlois, in which form he engenders Arthur upon Igrain. He later marries Igrain.

GROMER SOMER JOURE Brother of Ragnall who challenges Arthur with a riddle: 'What is it women most desire?' A powerful Otherworldly figure and enchanter, he is defeated by Arthur with the help of Gawain and confesses that he was himself enchanted by Morgan le Fay.

GUINEVERE Daughter of Leodegrance and wife of Arthur. Her affair with Lancelot brings down the kingdom, and she ends her days in the nunnery of Amesbury, where she is finally buried after taking a last leave of Lancelot. Her original role was as the Flower Bride, an ancient aspect of the Goddess whose function was to be fought over by

GARETH OF ORKNEY

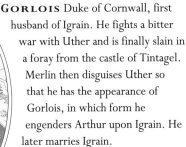

SIR
GAWAINE

the contending powers of summer and winter. At one time Arthur and Lancelot must have taken these roles.

IGRAIN Mother of Arthur. Tradition speaks of her as coming from Atlantis, but in most versions of the story she is the wife of Gorlois of Cornwall. Uther falls in love with Igrain, and through Merlin's enchantment he is given the likeness of Igrain's husband. Uther begets Arthur upon her.

ISOLT OF CORNWALL Born Isolt of Ireland, daughter of King Anguish of Ireland. She was the intended wife of Mark of Cornwall, but became the lover of Tristan after drinking a love potion intended for her wedding night. A famous beauty, also known as Belle Iseult, her affair with Tristan shocked the Arthurian court and drew attention for a time from the love of Lancelot and Guinevere. Arriving too late to save Tristan from a poisoned wound, she fell dead and was buried alongside him in Brittany.

ISOLT OF THE WHITE HANDS Daughter of the King of Brittany, she became Tristan's wife at the behest of her brother Kaherdin. The marriage was not consummated and Isolt became bitter towards her husband — finally bringing about his death by lying about the colour of the sails on the ship bringing Isolt of Cornwall to his aid. She committed suicide shortly after.

JOSEPH OF ARIMATHAEA Saint. A rich Jew with connections in the Cornish tin trade, he may have visited Britain with the young Jesus. Later, after the Crucifixion, he claimed the body of the Messiah and interred it in his own tomb. As a reward, he was later given custodianship of the Grail and founded a family of guardians

LADY
GUINEVERE

THE LADY BELLE ISEULT

who continued to watch over until the time of its achieving by Galahad, who was a direct descendant of Joseph. he is also credited with building the first Christian church, dedicated to the Virgin Mary, at Glastonbury in Somerset.

KAY Arthur's foster-brother, son of Ector. He became Arthur's Seneschal, and served him faithfully in this office until the end of the Round Table. His irascible nature and occasional cruelty earned him an unsympathetic reputation, but he was a good knight for all that and seems to have been genuinely loved by Arthur.

LAMORACK Son of Pellinore. One of the strongest Knights of the Round Table, he fell in love with Morgause and was finally murdered by Gawain and his brothers when he found their mother with Lamorack.

LANCELOT Son of King Ban of Benwick, sometimes called Lancelot du Lac, after his fostering in the Otherworldly realm of the Lake. He retained many qualities of the faery knight which enabled him to take his place as the most renowned of Arthur's knights. He took over from Gawain the role of queen's champion and fell in love with Guinevere. There are many stories which tell of Lancelot's prowess and his attempts to rid the kingdom of evil custom: in this guardianship of the land, he substitutes the kingly role of Arthur. After being tricked into sleeping with Elaine of Corbenic, he ran mad. After his healing, he took part in the Grail quest. Unable to attain the vessel himself, due to his adulterous love of Guinevere, he is represented and surpassed by Galahad his son. Eventually banished from court, he became a hermit after Arthur's passing.

LAMORACK

LANCELOT

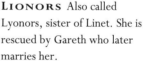

MERLIN

LOT King of Orkney and husband of Morgause. At the beginning of Arthur's reign, he was one of the rebel kings. The Orkney clan, consisting of his sons Gawain, Agravain, Gaheries and Gareth and their mother, retain some animosity towards Arthur's reign; though, ironically, it is in Mordred, the son of Morgause, by Arthur, that the seeds of former rebellion surface. He was killed by Pellinore.

LINET Sometimes called Lynette or Le Demoiselle Sauvage. Linet comes to court asking help for her imprisoned sister, Lionors or Lyonors. The only available knight is the recently knighted Beaumains – Gareth – whose chivalric inexperience she unmercifully taunts. She also appears in an earlier story as the guide and protector of Owein.

LIONORS Also called Lyonors, sister of Linet. She is rescued by Gareth who later marries her.

MARK King of Cornwall, uncle of Tristan whom he sends to obtain his bride, Isolt, daughter of the King of Ireland, with disastrous results for his own happiness. Isolt avoids her own wedding night by sending her companion, Brangaine, to Mark's bed. Mark is represented as a cuckold who condones Isolt's infidelity, though he frequently pursued the queen and his nephew.

MARK

MERLIN Magician and guardian of the Pendragon line. Born to a virgin who was visited by a spirit, Merlin Emrys was discovered by Vortigern's men as the perfect sacrifice to help seal the foundations of his tumbling-down tower. Merlin tells of the eternal battle between the dragons which underlie the foundations in a story which reflects the racial nature of this theme. He makes prophecies about Britain in

THE
ELEMENT
LIBRARY
THE
ARTHURIAN
TRADITION

gnomic verses and becomes the
advisor of Ambrosius
Aurelianus and his brother
Uther, in the course of whose
reign he magically builds
Stonehenge. Arthur inherits
Merlin as magical advisor for
only a short while. Merlin
returns to Arthur's father's
realm to become the eternal
guardian of Britain, according
to earlier sources, or succumbs
to the charms of Nimue,
according to later French
sources. Merlin is the chief
architect of the Pendragon's strategy and the
inner guardian of the land which, in early
times, was called Clas Merddin, or
Merlin's Enclosure.

MORDRED The incestuously begotten son
of Arthur and Morgause. When Arthur realised
that he had slept with his half-sister, he
attempted to kill his son by issuing a Herod-like
proclamation that all babies born at that time
be exposed in an open boat. Mordred survived
to be raised by Morgause who eventually sent
him to court, though Mordred was never
openly recognised as Arthur's son or successor.
When the Round Table was in collapse,
Mordred capitalised on the weakness of the
realm and Arthur's absence to seize command.
He was slain by Arthur, whom he
mortally wounded.

MORGAN LE FAY Daughter
of Gorlois and Igrain. She was
sent to a monastery, ostensibly
to be educated as a nun, though
she learned the magical arts.
She made a political match with
Uriens of Gore and became the
mother of Owein. Ever at
enmity with Arthur and his plans,
she seemed to be always plotting
some new enormity. However,
Morgan's role as protector of the
land led her to adopt some
challenging measures to keep
Arthur's kingship bright. Morgan has many
early and Celtic correlatives which make plain
the nature of her role as guardian of Britain's

MORDRED

MORGAN LE FAY

sovereignty, which she in many
ways embodies.

MORGAUSE Wife of Lot,
daughter of Igrain and Gorlois.
She was politically married to
Lot of Orkney, by whom she had
Gawain, Gaheries, Agravain and
Gareth. She bore Mordred to
Arthur after having seduced her
half-brother on the eve of his
coronation. She became
Lamorack's mistress and, on
being discovered in bed with
him, was slain by Gaheries.

MOROLD Isolt of Cornwall's
uncle, sometimes called Marhaus. Mark had to
pay a levy to Anguish of Ireland; when he
discontinued this payment, Morold was sent
out to fight Mark's champion Tristan, whom he
wounded severely and by whom he was slain.

NIMUE Sometimes also called Vivienne. She
was the daughter of Dionas, a gentleman who
was a votary of Diana. Nimue was conflated
with the Lady of the Lake in later Traditions.
Merlin taught her magic and eventually became
infatuated with her, according to Malory, so
that Nimue was able to entice and imprison him
under a great stone. She then adopted Merlin's
magical mantle throughout the rest of the story.

OWEIN Son of Morgan and Uriens,
sometimes called Ywain. Owein is one of the
earliest Arthurian knights and, in the
Mabiogion, becomes the husband of
the Lady of the Fountain and the
master of the Enchanted Games. In
later tradition, Owein prevents
Morgan from killing his father.
He rescues a lion which becomes
his companion and he is
sometimes called the Knight of
the Lion.

PALOMIDES Saracen knight,
in love with Isolt of Cornwall. He
became the pursuer of the
Questing Beast, after the death of
King Pellinore.

PELLES King of Corbenic and
member of the Grail Family. Also called
Pellam. Pelles was wounded with the Dolorous
Spear by Balin and so became the King of the

Waste Land, which could not be restored save by the Grail winner. Pelles condoned the use of magic to lure Lancelot to sleep with his daughter, Elaine of Corbenic, in order that this achiever of the Grail could be engendered and his land saved.

PELLINORE King Pellinore was the father of Perceval and Lamorack. His chief task was the pursuit of the Questing Beast. Because Pellinore had killed Lot, a long feud lay between the families of Pellinore and Orkney. Eventually Gawain and Gaheries slew Pellinore in revenge.

PERCEVAL Son of Pellinore, one of the Grail winners. According to most traditions, Perceval was raised by his mother in ignorance of arms and courtesy, but his natural prowess led him to Arthur's court where he immediately set off in pursuit of a knight who had insulted Guinevere. His further training in arms brought him into the hall of the Fisher King where he forbore to ask the all-healing Grail Question out of ill-placed courtesy. His subsequent quest and finding of the Grail is related in the earlier traditions, where he becomes the new Grail Guardian. However, later texts replace Perceval by Galahad as the Grail winner, Perceval here becomes Galahad's companion. Perceval's early ignorance has tagged him 'the Perfect Fool', but his is a Christ-like simplicity without offence which eventually develops and matures into real insight and wisdom.

RAGNALL Sister of Gromer. Enchanted into the shape of an ugly hag by Morgan, she comes to the rescue of Arthur who strives to find the answer to Gromer's riddle. She agrees to tell him the answer in return for her marriage to Gawain. Arthur accepts on Gawain's behalf. Gromer arrives and poses the question once more: 'What is it women most desire?' and Arthur relates the answer: 'Women desire to have sovereignty over men'. Gawain and Ragnall are wed and, at their first kiss, she is transformed into a beautiful maiden. However,

Gawain is asked to decide whether she shall be fair by day and foul by night, or the reverse. Fully realising the meaning of the riddle, Gawain begs her to choose and Ragnall is forever disenchanted.

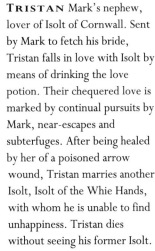

TRISTAN

TRISTAN Mark's nephew, lover of Isolt of Cornwall. Sent by Mark to fetch his bride, Tristan falls in love with Isolt by means of drinking the love potion. Their chequered love is marked by continual pursuits by Mark, near-escapes and subterfuges. After being healed by her of a poisoned arrow wound, Tristan marries another Isolt, Isolt of the Whie Hands, with whom he is unable to find unhappiness. Tristan dies without seeing his former Isolt. He is the truly bardic knight, without the pristine chivalry of Lancelot: a true Celt in his poetic love-making.

URIENS OF GORE One of the early rebels against Arthur, he remained one of Arthur's most faithful followers. He was father of Owein and husband of Morgan.

UTHER PENDRAGON Father of Arthur, second husband of Igrain. After becoming king, Uther saw Igrain and lusted for her. He lay siege to her husband, Gorlois' castle and, in his absence, and with the aid of Merlin, took on the shape of Gorlois in order to sleep with her. In the same hour Gorlois perished in battle. His taking of Igrain for himself, coupled with further hints in other texts, reveals him to have practised 'the Custom of the Pendragon' – a form of droit de seigneur.

VORTIGERN The predecessor of Ambrosius, he invited Saxon mercenaries into Britain in order to protect the realm: an action hardly popular among the people. His attempts to build a tower stronghold came to nothing, for it kept tumbling down. Counselled by his druids to sacrifice a boy without a father, Vortigern found Merlin. Merlin challenged his druids and then prophesied the fate of Britain. Vortigern died shortly after.

THE
ELEMENT
LIBRARY
THE
ARTHURIAN
TRADITION

BIBLIOGRAPHY

1. ANDREAS CAPELLANUS *The Art of Courtly Love*, trans. J.J. Parry, New York, Norton & Co., 1969.

2. ASHE, G. 'Merlin in the Earliest Records', in *The Book of Merlin*, ed. R.J. Stewart, Poole, Blandford Press, 1987.

3. BEROUL, *The Romance of Tristan*, trans. A. S. Frederick, Penguin Books, 1970.

4. BRADLEY, M.Z., *The Mists of Avalon*, Michael Joseph, 1983.

5. BRADSHAW, G., *Down the Long Wind*, Methuen, 1988.

6. BROMWICH, R., *Triodd Ynys Prydein*, Cardiff, University of Wales Press, 1978.

7. CHAMBERS, A.K., *Arthur of Britain*, Sidgewick & Jackson, 1927.

8. CHRÉTIEN DE TROYES, *Arthurian Romances*, trans. D.D.R. Owen, Dent, 1987.

9. *Le Chevalier de Papegau*, ed. & trans. T.E. Vesce, New York, Garland Publishing, 1986.

10. CROSS, T.P. & SLOVER, C.H., *Ancient Irish Tales*, Dublin Figgis, 1936.

11. DANTE ALIGHIERI, *The Divine Comedy*, trans. Lawrence Binyon, Agenda Editions, 1979.

12. DE ROUGEMONT, D., *Love in the Western World*, New York, Pantheon, 1969.

13. EISNER, S., *The Tristan Legend*, Illinois, Northwestern University Press, 1969.

14. EVANS, S., *In Quest of the Holy Grail*, J.M. Dent, 1898.

15. FORTUNE, D., *Avalon of the Heart*, Wellingborough, Aquarian Press, 1971.

16. FRANKLAND, E., *The Bear of Britain*, Macdonald, 1941.

17. FRANZ, M.L.& C.G. Jung: *His Myth in Our Time*, Hodder & Stoughton, 1975.

18. GARDNER, J.,*The Complete Works of the Gawain Poet*, Southern Illinois University Press, 1965.

19. GASTER, M., 'The Legend of Merlin', *Folklore* 16 (1905).

20. GEOFFREY OF MONMOUTH, *The History of the Kings of Britain*, trans. Lewis Thorpe, Penguin, 1966.

21. GEOFFREY OF MONMOUTH, *The Vita Merlini*, trans J.J. Parry, University of Illinois, 1925.

22. GOTTFRIED VON STRASSBOURG, *Tristan*, trans. A. T. Chatto, Penguin Books, 1967.

23. HALL, L.B., *The Knightly Tales of Sir Gawain*, Chicago, Ill., Nelson Hall, 1976.

24. HEATH-STUBBS, J., *Artorius*, Enitharmon Press, 1974.

25. JOHNSON, R.A., *The Psychology of Romantic Love*, Routledge & Kegan Paul, 1983.

26. JONES, D.E.F., *The English Spirit*, Rudolf Steiner Press, 1982.

27. JONES, D., *The Anathemata*, Faber, 1952.

28. JONES, E., *In Parenthesis*, Faber, 1937.

29. JONES, D., *The Sleeping Lord*, Faber, 1974.

30. KARR, P.A., *The King Arthur Companion,* Albany, Chaosium Inc., 1983.

31. KENNEDY, B., *Knighthood in the Morte D'Arthur*, Cambridge, D.S. Brewer, 1986.

32. KNIGHT, G., 'The Archetype of Merlin', in *The Book of Merlin*, ed. R.J. Stewart, Poole, Blandford Press, 1987.

33. KNIGHT, G., *The Magical World of the Inklings*, Shaftesbury, Element Books, 1991.

34. KNIGHT, G., *The Secret Tradition in Arthurian Legend*, Wellingborough, Aquarian Press, 1983.

35. LACY, N.J. & ASHE, G., *The Arthurian Handbook*, New York, Garland Publishing Inc., 1988.

36. *Lancelot of the Lake*, trans. C. Corley, Oxford University Press, 1989.

37. *Lanzalet*, trans. K.G.T. Webster, New York, Columbia University Press, 1951.

38. LAWHEAD, S., *Arthur*, Lion Books, 1989.

39. LAWHEAD, S., *Merlin*, Lion Books, 1988.

40. LAWHEAD, S., *Taliesin*, Lion Books, 1988.

41. LIEVERGOOD, B.C.J., *Mystery Streams in Europe and the New Mysteries*, New York, The Anthroposopic Press, 1982.

42. LOFFLER, C.M., *The Voyage to the Otherworld Island in Early Irish Literature*, 2 vols., Universität Salzburg, 1983.

43. LOOMIS, R.S., *The Development of Arthurian Romance*, New York, Norton, 1963.

44. LOOMIS, R.S., *The Grail From Celtic Myth to Christian Symbolism*, University of Wales Press/Columbia University Press, 1963.

45. LOOMIS, R.S., *Wales & the Arthurian Legend*, Folcroft Library Editions, 1977.

46. *The Mabinogion*, trans. J. Gantz, Penguin Books, 1976.

47. MALORY, Sir Thomas, *Le Morte D'Arthur*, New York, University Books, 1961.

48. MARIE DE FRANCE, *Lais*, trans. G.S. Burgess and K. Busby, Harmondsworth, Penguin Books, 1986.

49. MARKALE, J., *King Arthur: King of Kings*, Gordon Cremonesi, 1977.

50. MARKALE, J., *Women of the Celts*, Gordon Cremonesi, 1975.

51. MASEFIELD, J., *Midsummer Night*, Heinemann,1928.

52. MATTHEWS, C., *Arthur and the Sovereignty of Britain*, Arkana, 1989.

53. MATTHEWS, C., *Mabon and the Mysteries of Britain*, Arkana, 1987.

54. MATTHEWS, C., *Elements of the Celtic Tradition*, Shaftesbury, Element Books, 1989.

55. MATTHEWS, 'An Awesome & Splendid Thing That We Did', *Quadriga* 19 (Autumn, 1981).

56. MATTHEWS, C. & J., *The Arthurian Tarot: A Hallowquest*, Aquarian Press, 1990.

57. MATTHEWS, J., *An Arthurian Reader*, Wellingborough, Aquarian Press, 1988.

58. MATTHEWS, J., *Elements of the Grail Tradition*, Shaftesbury, Element Books, 1990.

59. MATTHEWS, J., *Gawain, Knight of the Goddess*, Wellingborough, Aquarian Press, 1990.

60. MATTHEWS, J., *Taliesin: Shamanic Mysteries in Britain and Ireland*, Unwin Hyman, 1990.

62. MATTHEWS, J., and STEWART, R.J., *Warriors of Arthur*, Poole, Blandford Press, 1987.

63. MERRY, E., *The Flaming Door*, Edinburgh, Floris, 1983.

64. PATON, L.A., *Studies in the Fairy Mythology of Arthurian Romance*, New York, Franklin, 1959.

65. PAXSON, D.L., *The White Raven*, New York, William Morrow, 1988.

66. POWYS, J.C., *Porius*, Village Press, 1974.

67. *Quest of the Holy Grail*, trans. P.M. Matarasso, Penguin Books, 1969.

68. RHYS, J., *Studies in the Arthurian Legend*, Oxford University Press, 1891.

69. SHAVER, A., *Tristan and the Round Table*, New York, Medieval and Renaissance Texts & Studies, 1983.

70. SKEELES, D., *The Romance of Perceval in Prose*, Seattle, University of Washington Press, 1966.

71. SOMMER, H.O., *The Vulgate Version of the Arthurian Romances*, 7 vols., Washington, The Carnegie Institution, 1909-16.

72. STEWART, M., *The Crystal Cave,* Hodder & Stoughton, 1970.

73. STEWART, M. *The Hollow Hills*, Hodder & Stoughton, 1973.

74. STEWART, M., *The Last Enchantment*, Hodder & Stoughton, 1979.

75. STEWART, R.J. (ed.), *The Book of Merlin*, Poole, Blandford Press, 1987.

76. STEWART, R.J., (ed.), *Merlin and Women*, Blandford Press, 1986.

77. STEWART, R.J., *The Mystic Life of Merlin*, Arkana, 1986.

78. STEWART, R.J., *The Prophetic Vision of Merlin*, Arkana, 1986.

79. STEWART, R.J., & MATTHEWS, J., *Legendary Britain*, Poole, Blandford Press, 1989.

80. SUTCLIFF, R., *The Sword at Sunset*, Hodder & Stoughton, 1963.

81. THOMAS, *Tristan in Brittany*, trans. D. L. Sayers, 1929.

82. TENNYSON, A., *Idylls of the King*, Penguin Books, 1983.

83. TOLSTOY, N., *The Quest for Merlin*, Hamish Hamilton, 1986.

84. TRAVERS, P.L., *What the Bee Knows*, Wellingborough, Aquarian Press, 1989.

85. TREECE, H., *The Great Captains*, Savoy Books, 1980.

86. VON FRANZ, M.L.& *C.G. Jung: His Myth in Our Time*, Hodder & Stoughton, 1972.

87. WAY, G.LK., *Fabliaux or Tales*, Rodwell, 1815.

88. WESTON, J.L., 'The Esplumoir of Merlin', Speculum, 1946.

89. WESTON, J.L., *The Legend of Sir Perceval*, David Nutt, 1909.

90. WHITE, T.H., *The Once and Future King*, Collins, 1958.

91. WHITE, T.H., *The Book of Merlyn*, Collins, 1978.

92. WILLIAMS, C., *Taliesin Through Logres, The Region of the Summer Stars, Arthurian Torso*, Michigan, Erdmans, 1974.

THE
ELEMENT
LIBRARY
THE
ARTHURIAN
TRADITION

ARTHURIAN JOURNALS
AND SOCIETIES

The rates quoted are correct at the time of publication.
Please send an SAE or international reply-paid coupon for
further details.

Quondam et Futurus, Henry Hall Peyton III and Bonnie Wheeler Eds.
English Dept. Memphis State University, Memphis, TN 38152,
USA. (A quarterly journal of Arthurian interpretations. Good
scholarly essays with some lighter material. One of the best
Arthurian journals currently available. Subscription: $30 in USA,
$40 elsewhere.)

Pendragon, Fred Steadman-Jones Ed. Smithy House, Newton by
Frodsham, Cheshire, WA6 68X. (Journal of the Pendragon Society.
A lively forum for Arthurian discussion and news. Occasional
events. Quarterly publication. Send SAE for subscription details).

Hallowquest Newsletter is issued quarterly, giving details of events,
books, tapes and courses by Caitlín & John Matthews. Current
subscription rates: £3.50 in UK and £10 or $15 US dollars or 25
international reply paid coupons overseas. Sterling cheques
payable to *Graal Publications,* BCM HALLOWQUEST, London
WC1N 3XX.

The International Arthurian Society, Secretary/Treasurer Dr
Geoffrey Bromiley, Dept of French, Univ. of Durham, Elvet
Riverside, New Elvet, Durham DH1 3JT. (This is the main
Arthurian society in the world to which all Arthurian scholars
subscribe. It holds a biennial conference and produces a
bibliographical bulletin every year.)

ACKNOWLEDGEMENTS

By Permission of Birmingham Museums and Art Gallery
6, 41, 43t, 55b, 79b

The Bodleian Library, Oxford (MS Douce 383) 11t;
(MS Douce 178) 22, 25, 28, 64t; (MS Douce 215) 33t

Cameron Collection 7b, 8, 8–9, 9b, 15t, 16, 17, 19t, 21t,
21b, 23, 27, 33b, 34t, 34b, 36b, 37t, 37b, 38b, 42, 43b, 45b,
56, 61, 63t, 63b, 69b, 71b, 80l

Fine Art Photographic Library 10, 21, 35, 44, 46, 50, 57b,
57bl, 60, 73

Fortean Picture Library: JANET AND COLIN BORD 12t,
12b, 15b, 24–5, 26b, 68t, 72, 74; PAUL BROADHURST 13, 14,
81r; ROGER VLITOS 84

P Kent 32, 54

King Arthur's Great Halls, Tintagel 7t, 55t, 62, 69t, 86, 89

**Laing Art Gallery, Newcastle-upon-Tyne (Tyne and
Wear Museums)** 26t, 76

**Courtesy Kobal Collection,
Orion/Warner Bros** 83

Stuart Littlejohn, 45t

Manchester City Art Galleries 85 (James Archer:
La Mort D'Arthur)

The Mansell Collection 67

Mary Evans Picture Library 19b, 29, 40, 48, 57br, 59b,
65t, 68b, 75

Spectrum Colour Library 39b, 58

By Permission of the Trustees of the Tate Gallery 66,
78 and front cover

**By Courtesy of the Board of Trustees of the
Victoria and Albert Museum** 30

**By Kind Permission of the Trustees of the David Jones
Estate** 81 (TRISTAN), 82 (HE FREES THE WATERS).

INDEX

A

Aglovale 39
Agravain 39, 82
apple trees 27, 30, 75
Arawn 17, 45, 46
Archer, James 84
archetypes 18, 19, 20, 36, 70
    Avalon 77
    esoteric principles 84
    Round Table 85
Arderydd, battle of 27
The Art of Courtly Love 60
Arthur, King 36
    archetype 84—5
    Avalon 75
    fame 8—9
    Grail Quest 67
    history 11—13
    literature 81
    love 51, 54—5
    mythology 18—21
    Otherworld 73
    resting place 74
    return of 78—85
    romantic tradition 14—18
    symbolism 69
    Tristan 58
Atlantis 83
Avalon 10—11, 20, 36, 45, 55
    faery realms 72—7
    literature 83

B

Badon, battle of 12—13
Ban, King 22, 52—3
Beardsley, Aubrey 24
Bede 25
Bedivere 17
Bernard of Clairvaux 30, 67
Blake, William 79
Boorman, John 83
Borron, Robert de 28, 40,
    64, 67

Bors 22, 70
Bradley, Marion Zimmer 82—83
Bradshaw, Gillian 82, 83
Bran 17, 44, 63, 73
Brangane 57
Britons 13, 23, 72
Brittany 13, 58
Burne-Jones, Edward 79, 80

C

Calidon 56
Camelot 22—31, 43, 53, 70, 74
Camlan, battle of 19, 40, 42,
    74—5, 81—2
Carl of Carlisle 73
Cauldron 63, 75, 76
Caxton, William 18
Celts 11, 13, 16—17, 20, 44
    apple trees 27
    Cauldron 63
    Hades 46
    Iberian 52
    love 51
    Otherworld 73, 74, 75
    shamanism 28
Ceridwen 63
Cervantes, Miguel 79, 80
Chaucer, Geoffrey 20
chivalry 8, 34—5, 39, 47, 50—61
Chrétien de Troyes 9, 47, 61,64
Christianity 28—9, 31, 38, 40,42
    Arthurian legends 44—5
    Grail Quest 67—8, 70, 71
Churchyard, Thomas 79
Cistercian monks 30, 67, 68
Constantine 14, 25, 26
Courtly Love see love
Crowley, Aleister 84
Crusades 67
Cuchulainn 17, 76

D

Dante 54

Dark Ages 14, 81
Dark Goddess 44-5
de Galles clan 39, 40
Don Quixote 79, 80
dragons 23, 38
druids 23, 24, 26, 29

E

Ector 53, 55
Elaine of Astolat 9, 54, 61
Elaine of Corbenic 54, 56
Eleanor, Queen of Aquitaine
    39, 60
Elisabeth, Queen 56
Elizabeth I, Queen of England
    79, 80
enchantresses 17, 19, 41—9, 56
English race 13
Excalibur 20, 21, 83

F

The Faerie Queene 79, 80
faery realms 72—7
Fellowship of the Round Table
    33-6, 38—40, 43, 53
    Avalon 74, 77
    Grail Quest 69
Flower Bride 45—6, 68
forests 35—40
Fortune, Dion 63, 76, 83, 84
François, King of France 34
Frankland, Edward 81

G

Gaheries 39, 54, 82
Galahad 21, 53, 54, 66, 67—8
    Avalon 76
    Grail Quest 70, 71
    Round Table 69
Ganeida 29, 31
Gareth 39, 48, 54, 82

Gawain 39, 43—4, 46, 48—9, 51
    Grail Quest 64
    Green Knight 31
    literature 17, 20, 82, 83
    love 61
    Otherworld 35, 73
    Round Table 34
Geoffrey of Monmouth 14—15,
    23—7, 42, 75, 83
Geraint 41
Gesta Regum Britanniae 75
Giant's Dance 25, 40
Glastonbury, Somerset 68,
    74, 84
Governal 56
Grail Quest 62—71
Greek mythology 76—7
Green Knight 31, 49
Guerrehes 33
guides 41
Guigomar 16
Guinevere, Queen 16, 18,
    32, 35—6, 45—6
    archetypes 84
    literature 82
    love 51, 53, 54—6, 59, 61
    symbolism 69

H

Hades 46
Henry VII, King of England 79
Hesperides 77
Holy Grail 16, 21, 28, 31,
    38—40
    Courtly Love 60, 61
    Gawain 43
    Glastonbury 74
    Lancelot 55
    literature 82
    Otherworld 73
    Quest 62—71
    spirituality 61
    symbolism 83

THE
ELEMENT
LIBRARY
THE
ARTHURIAN
TRADITION

ᴵ I ᴵ

Igrain 11, 42, 83
immortality 63
Inklings 82
Inquisition 67
Isolt 51, 56–9, 81

ᴶ J ᴶ

James I, King of England and
        VI of Scotland 79
Jerusalem 67
Jesus Christ 64, 65, 66
Jones, David 80, 85
Jonson, Ben 79
Joseph of Arimathaea 64, 65,
        66, 68
    Glastonbury 74
    Otherworld 73
Jung, Carl 31

ᴷ K ᴷ

Kai 17
Knight, Gareth 82, 84

ᴸ L ᴸ

Lady of the Lake 30, 51, 53
Lailoken 29
Lamorack 39
Lancelot 16–18, 20, 45–8,
        50–61
    Avalon 76
    Elaine 9
    Grail Quest 69
    literature 82
    Round Table 69
    Tristan 58
Last Supper 40
Launfal 36
Lawhead, Stephen 82, 83
Le Morte D'Arthur 8, 18,
        30, 47, 81
    chivalry 60
    Grail Quest 69
Leodegrance, King 33, 53
Lewis, C.S. 82
Lot, King 39, 48
love 50–61
Lugh 19

Lull, Ramon 39
Lynette 47, 48

ᴹ M ᴹ

Mabinogion 9, 16, 18, 41,
        45, 52
magicians 17
Malory, Thomas 8–9, 18, 21,
        60, 81
    Avalon 75
    chivalry 39
    goddesses 42, 47
    Grail Quest 70
Manus 37
Marie de France 38, 39, 47
Mark, King of Cornwall 56–9
Markale, Jean 17, 77
Masefield, John 82
Meliodas, King 56
Merlin 11, 14, 21, 40, 52
    archetypes 84
    Avalon 75
    literature 79, 81, 82, 83
    Otherworld 73
    prophecies 22–31, 33, 79
    Questing Beast 36
    Round Table 20
Milton, John 79
Mordred 9, 19, 39, 44, 69
    Guinevere 45
    literature 81, 82
    Round Table Fellowship 54
Morgan le Fay 19, 20, 42–3,
        44, 45
    archetypes 84
    Avalon 74–5
    literature 83
Morgause 39, 44, 48, 69
    literature 82
Morrighan 42, 45
Morris, William 79, 80
mythology, Greek 76–7

ᴺ N ᴺ

necromancy 28, 29, 42
Nennius 25
New Testament 68
Nimue 30–1, 51, 65, 75

ᴼ O ᴼ

Order of the Golden Dawn 83
Orkney clan 39, 40
Otherworld 16, 17, 19, 35–40, 42
    dream of 73
    Grail Quest 71
    love 51–2, 61

ᴾ P ᴾ

Pallenburg, Rospo 83
Palomides 36
Paxon, Diana 83
Pelles, King 54
Pellinore, King 34, 36, 39
Perceval 39, 64, 65, 70
Picts 23, 52
Powys, John Cowper 81
Pre–Raphaelites 79, 80
prophecies 22–31
Pwyll 45, 46

ᴼ Q ᴼ

Questing Beast 36

ᴿ R ᴿ

Ragnall 20, 36, 49
ravens 19
Rhydderch, King 29
Romans 12
Romanticism 79
Round Table 15, 32–40, 43, 53
    archetypes 85
    Avalon 74, 77
    Grail Quest 69

ˢ S ˢ

St Gildas 16
St Kentigern 29
St Patrick 74
Saracens 36
Saxons 12, 13, 23
shamanism 24, 27, 28, 29, 37
shape–shifting 42
Sir Gawain and the Green Knight
        43, 45
Skene W.F. 27
Society of the Inner Light 84

Spenser, Edmund 79, 80
spirituality 62–71
stags 16, 28, 29
Stewart, Mary 82, 83
Stewart, R.J. 24, 29, 84
Stone of Merlin 31
Stonehenge 25, 26, 40
Strassbourg, Gottfried von 60–1
Stubbs, John Heath 82
Sufis 63
Sutcliff, Rosemary 81

ᵀ T ᵀ

Taliesin 27, 29, 82
tarot cards 29
Tennyson, Alfred Lord 61,
        68, 79, 85
Thirteen Treasures of Britain 73
Tintagel Cornwall 26
Tolkien J.R.R. 82
Tor 39
Travers, P.L. 54
Travers, Pamela 8
Treece, Henry 81
Tristan 50–1, 56–61, 81, 83
troubadors 50, 52, 60, 61

ᵁ U ᵁ

Uther Pendragon, King 11,
        26, 33

ⱽ V ⱽ

Virgil 29
Vortigern 23, 25

ᵂ W ᵂ

Wace 15, 32
Waite A.E. 84
Walter Archdeacon of
        Oxford 25
weaponry 17, 20, 21
White, T.H. 81, 82
Williams, Charles 68, 82, 83

ʸ Y ʸ

Yeats, W.B. 84